HOW TO WRITE AND SELL
MYSTERY FICTION

How to Write and Sell Mystery Fiction

Edited by SYLVIA K. BURACK

Publishers   THE WRITER, INC.   *Boston*

"How to Keep the Reader on the Edge of the Chair," Copyright © 1973, by Joan Aiken

"Building Without Blueprints," Copyright © 1985, by Tony Hillerman

"One Clue at a Time, by P. D. James. Copyright © 1983 by *The New York Times.* Reprinted by permission.

Library of Congress Cataloging-in-Publication Data

How to write and sell mystery fiction / edited by Sylvia K. Burack.
   p. cm.
Includes bibliographical references.
ISBN 0-87116-162-1 : $12.95 (est.)
   1. Detective and mystery stories—authorship. I. Kamerman, Sylvia E.
PN3377.5.D4H6 1990
808.3'872—dc20   90-30109
                                           CIP

Printed in the United States of America

CONTENTS

HOW TO WRITE AND SELL MYSTERY FICTION

1

HOW TO KEEP THE READER ON THE EDGE OF THE CHAIR
by *Joan Aiken*

> Is the night chilly and dark?
> The night is chilly, but not dark.
> The thin grey cloud is spread on high
> It covers, but not hides, the sky.

OBSERVE HOW CUNNINGLY Coleridge sets the scene for something nasty to happen. He understates. He plays down. Nothing *seems* very bad; but as one small, carefully qualified detail is added to another, each harmless in itself, the reader begins to notice a feeling of menace; there is an unusual element about the almost obsessive moderateness of every assertion that Coleridge is making. The cock crows, but it crows drowsily; even the mastiff bitch, woken by the castle clock, makes answer in "sixteen short howls, not over loud." Coleridge is anxious to pretend that everything is quite normal, but he lets us see that he is pretending too hard.

> The moon is behind, and at the full
> And yet she seems both small and dull
> 'Tis a month before the month of May
> And spring comes slowly up this way . . .

He is almost apologetic about it. There is no storm, no drama; everything is very subdued; everything can be accounted for; nothing is wrong—not *exactly*.

> She stole along; she nothing spoke
> The sighs she heaved were soft and low
> And nought was green upon the oak
> But moss and rarest mistletoe . . .

Presently this very moderation, this very understatement, begins to play on the reader's nerves. All the negatives create an atmosphere of tension, of expectation.

> The night is chill; the forest bare
> Is it the wind that moaneth bleak?
> There is not wind enough in the air
> To move away the ringlet curl
> From the lovely lady's cheek . . .

The lovely lady is Christabel, gone out to pray for her lover in the midnight forest. The trappings are pure gothic: the remote forest hall (somewhere in the English Lake District; the names Dungeon Ghyll and Witch's Lair are later irrelevantly tossed in for a bit of gratuitous creepiness), the night scene and the unsuspecting simple-hearted heroine whose betrothed knight is off at the wars and not available to protect her—all are staple ingredients of the contemporary gothic novel. Coleridge gets down to business at once. In the midnight wood, Christabel finds a woebegone lady who tells a cock-and-bull story of having been abducted by five ravishers on white steeds; innocent Christabel hospitably leads home the lady, who loses no time in putting the come-hither on Sir Leoline the Baron rich. But things look bad for Christabel; the strange lady's eyes turn to serpents' eyes when she looks at the poor girl, who straightway falls under a hypnotic spell and can't reveal the sinister knowledge she has acquired about the visitor. Meanwhile, the only possible ally, Bracy the bard, has been dispatched in search of the lady's father, who is alleged to live a long way off on the Scottish border.

The scene is set for dark doings at Langdale Hall, in fact. A paperback blurb for one of my novels (and a few thousand others)—"Who was trying to enslave her body and destroy her mind? She woke to Terror . . ."—would do equally well for Christabel.

Unfortunately, we shall never know what was to happen to her, for Coleridge (though the person from Porlock doesn't seem to have been responsible this time) did not finish the poem. But what a good beginning it is: a first-class example of how an atmosphere of horror and anticipation can be achieved, not by loud bangs and vampire shrieks, but by a series of careful, gentle touches.

Henry James achieves the same effect in *The Turn of the Screw.* If you analyze that story, remarkably little actually takes place: Two ghosts are seen from time to time; sometimes a man staring through a window, sometimes a woman gazing steadily across a lake. But what a power these apparitions have. Part of their horror lies in the silent suddenness with which they appear and disappear—no spooky atmosphere preliminaries, just the flat event itself, unnerving as a blown fuse. "There again, against the glass . . . was the hideous author of our woe—the white face of damnation." "She rose erect on the spot my friend and I had lately quitted." Very much of the horror, too, lies in the moderate, reasonable tone in which the whole story is told.

Frightening your reader

Both Henry James and Coleridge were accomplished professionals; both knew just what they were about. It is interesting that in each of these examples the writer can be seen quite consciously and deliberately making it plain that he is out to scare the reader, right from the start. Coleridge does it in his opening lines:

'Tis the middle of night by the castle clock
And the owls have awakened the crowing cock
Tu-whit—Tu-whoo . . . .

Midnight—castle—owl calls: The sequence is as good as a key-signature to indicate that the reader must be prepared for supernatural occurrences. Henry James does it even more directly; by his formal story-within-a-story framework, he gives himself the chance of announcing in advance that his tale is a horrible one, that it concerns the fate of two children, so that the reader is put into a receptive frame of mind. (If not in a receptive frame of mind, presumably he shuts the book.)

So the first step in frightening your reader is to *tell* him that you are going to frighten him—though not in terms so specific as to impair the effect of the fright itself when it finally arrives. (Relative to this, I have had one or two arguments with publishers, some of whom have a disastrous habit of giving away far too much plot in a thriller blurb: "At the end of a long and gripping chase the heroine discovers that the children have been safe all the time at the house of a neighbor," one blurb blithely revealed, raising my blood pressure to a dangerous level, since the heroine's uncertainty and terror about her children formed the whole fulcrum of my lever for keeping the reader up in the air.)

Tell your reader; then give him some idea what is in store.

"Hale knew, before he had been in Brighton three hours that they meant to murder him," Graham Greene begins *Brighton Rock*. And by page 23, sure enough, Hale has been murdered, not crudely in front of the reader, but offstage. The knowledge that his death has been so easily, so speedily arranged, is a kind of salesman's sample, a demonstration of what may yet occur to other characters.

I opened one of my thrillers with the sentence, "Hari Lupac was waiting for the girl he was going to murder," and then went on edging my way up to this murder for the whole book, ending with the girl's escape in the last line. I don't think it's my best book, though it's hard to judge the fright-content of one's own suspense stories—to oneself the mechanism shows so plainly—but several readers have told me they found that one really frightening.

Distinguishing suspense from horror

The early warning may occur obliquely. Le Fanu's *Uncle Silas,* another prototype gothic, starts well in tradition, with the secluded country mansion. "It was winter . . . great gusts were rattling at the windows . . . fire blazing in a sombre old room." Things don't really start to go wrong until the arrival of the sinister governess, Madame de la Rougierre, who is first seen outside the window in the moonlight, "curtseying extraordinarily low and rather fantastically." Sinister hints about Uncle Silas then begin to be dropped; Maud's father keeps insisting that his brother has been unjustly accused, Cousin Monica reveals that he was suspected of a murder. Furthermore, she gives a warning to Maud not to let the governess tamper with her food and vehemently objects to the arrangement whereby, at her father's death, Maud is sent to live with Uncle Silas, heir to the estate should Maud die before coming of age. Anyone but the heroine of a gothic would take fright, but not Maud, not even when she meets Uncle Silas, with his gentle, cold voice, long hair of the purest silver, face like marble, thin-lipped smile, and habitual contraction resembling a scowl—a classic wicked uncle if ever there was one—not even then does she lose her simple trust.

Uncle Silas has some gripping moments, but I find *The Turn of the Screw* infinitely more frightening, because the threat remains indefinite. The final twist, both in *The Turn of the Screw* and "Christabel," lies in the reader's total uncertainty as to what can possibly happen; in each case an evil supernatural force is in pursuit of an innocent victim, but what can this sinister power actually do? The writer doesn't say, and it is the sense of nameless menace, unformulated threat, that really has power to chill the blood. Demonic possession is a terrifying conception, and it is this that both stories are hinting at, but in each case the suggestion is kept, as it were, tucked up the writer's sleeve. This keeping back, this fear of the unknown, is what differentiates suspense from horror. Horror is specific, fear is indefinite. I don't at all decry the horror-genre but I personally find suspense more interesting, both to read and to write; also more of a challenge.

Suspense unlimited

Once you have prepared your reader to have his hair raised, the range of possible suspense is unlimited. But there are various tried and reliable threat situations—the failed rescue, for instance. *Uncle Silas* has a good example of this, when the scheming uncle sends away honest Doctor Bryerly, who realizes Maud's danger and tries to extricate her: "I heard that dismallest of sounds, the retreating footsteps of a true friend, *lost*." An even better example occurs in a short story by Michael Joyce, "Perchance to Dream": the hero is trapped in a dark house with his mad brother-in-law, a chemist who has been conducting sinister experiments on his wife and child. The police are summoned, but they arrive too late, the madman has run amok with an ax and is lurking in the front hall. So the police, after vainly knocking, *go away again*; it is a terrible moment when the hero realizes that he is not going to be able to summon them back.

A variation of this, sometimes a stage later in time, is the exposure of an appeal for help; up to this moment hero and villain have been conducting their maneuvers with a pretense of amity, without the admission that their interests are opposed, the villain gradually gaining ascendancy. Then, the hero (or heroine) sends out a help call. Maud, for instance, sends a message to her cousin, which is intercepted: "[Uncle Silas] rose like a spectre with a white scowl. 'Then how do you account for that?' he shrieked, smiting my open letter, face upward upon the table."

I used this device in my children's novel, *The Wolves of Willoughby Chase*. In it, the orphans appeal to their father's lawyer for help; their letter is intercepted by the wicked governess. Some readers have told me they found this a "bad moment." This comes partly, I think, from having the orphans found out and partly from the concept, "now she (the governess) *knows* I know how wicked she is," which for some psychological reason is always particularly frightening.

Hero/heroine discovered by villain in a compromising situation is always a moment of acute tension. In *Appointment with Yesterday,* Celia Fremlin has a woman sorting through old newspapers. She looks up and realizes that her husband is watching her through the window. A simple-sounding scene, but it has power to frighten you down to your socks. Why? Celia Fremlin has used plot-inversion to heighten suspense: The author opens the book with her heroine on the run, evidently fleeing from some appalling denouement relating to her husband. Then, in a series of flashbacks alternated with the chronological progress of the plot, the story returns to the start of the marriage. Miss Fremlin can be as leisurely as she pleases in the build-up of tension; she is confident of the reader's confidence in *her.*

Villains

Stevenson, who was a master hand at creating fear situations, made use of two infallible ingredients in *Treasure Island*—a child, and a crippled villain. Indeed, *Treasure Island* has two villains with physical disabilities, Blind Pew, whose entry into the book is a most terrifying scene, and Long John Silver. Why should a disabled villain be more frightening than one with all his faculties intact? I suppose it must be some atavistic streak in us: we perhaps feel that a physically handicapped person may have developed super-normal powers, may be a warlock, may feel supernormal malice and vindictiveness because of his physical inferiority. Or—Freudians would say—we fear him because we are afraid of being overtaken by the same misfortune; it is a castration fear. Whatever the reason, handicapped villains have held the stage from classic times: the one-eyed Cyclops, lame Vulcan, Richard Crookback (used by Shakespeare in *Richard III* and also by Stevenson in *The Black Arrow*), one-handed Captain Hook, one-legged Long John, Castro in Conrad's *Romance*. Mary Stewart has one of her villains (in *Nine Coaches Waiting*) confined to a wheelchair. The villain of *Jamaica Inn* is an albino. In one of Stevenson's most terrifying scenes, two boys are pursued by a blind leper; the combination of blindness and leprosy is almost too bloodcurdling. And yet, if one could be rational about it, what could a blind leper, what could a man in a wheelchair actually do? But one can't think it over rationally; that is the worst part of it. A Jekyll-Hyde personality split, or a moronic villain, as in James Hadley Chase's *No Orchids for Miss Blandish,* or in William Faulkner's *Sanctuary,* are all terrifying and unpredictable. But a writer should be sparing with mad villains; the temptation to make them go off the rails at the end of the novel is partly a kind of laziness. The villain is being bested, but the writer wants him to battle on as long as possible, against whatever odds. It is more ethical, though harder work, to have the villain defiant on logical grounds, not just a crazy refusal to give in.

A child villain or a senile villain can be equally terrifying. Truman Capote created an appalling little girl in Miriam. In *The Man Who Was Thursday,* G. K. Chesterton has a horrifying, dilapidated old man whose power to terrify lay in the fact that, although he seemed so old he was almost falling to bits, he could nevertheless manage to keep chasing the hero; supernatural fear again. (In fact Chesterton was cheating, because his old man turned out to be a young man in disguise, but it was a good fright while it lasted.)

Of course, an essential ingredient in a fear situation is a central character with whom the reader can empathize. A child is excellent, as Henry James demonstrated in *The Turn of the Screw,* or a defenseless person, such as the paralyzed heroine in Hilda Lawrence's *Duet for Four Hands;* or an old, incapable person—the old blind man in Elizabeth Fenwick's *A Friend for Mary Rose.* Hugh Walpole, in *Kind Lady,* has a masterly example in the old woman terrorized by the gang. This is also an example of the "enclosed-world" fear situation. The enclosed world can be literal: an island, a prison, an old people's home, an asylum, an occupied country; or it may be cut off not by physical barriers but mental ones. Moral subjugation can achieve this, or straight threat—a protection racket, for instance, where the enclosed world appears to form part of the world at large, but the barriers are really set up by the central character's fear of reprisals if he tries to appeal for help.

Graham Greene's Brighton is an enclosed world. So is the whole world in *The Man Who Was Thursday,* the whole of England in Wilkie Collins' *The Woman in White.* Chesterton and Wilkie Collins achieve their effects by apparently omniscient, omnipresent villains, who seem to have total knowledge of what their opponents are likely to do next; but readers now are more skeptical of this device than they were in the nineteenth century.

Creating fear

These are all technical ways of creating suspense, but there are two basic essentials without which I am sure it is impossible to create a really convincing fear situation. The first is conflict between good and evil. Fear situations are fundamentally primitive and simple. As soon as the conflict shifts to a different level, to disputed loyalty, for instance, or betrayal, or choice of allegiance, the issues become more sophisticated, and fear is replaced by anxiety.

The second essential is that at some point, no matter how long ago, the writer must in some degree have felt this fear himself. Writing is on a par with acting. The actor can't, obviously, feel the emotion all the time he is portraying it, but he must act out of experience; he must have the capacity to feel or he won't convince. In the same way, the writer will fail to frighten his reader unless he really knows what he is talking about.

Fear is not the only suspense situation. Hope is another. Will the pilot be able to land the crippled plane? Will the supplies arrive in time? Will the gas leak be discovered before it is too late? Will the prisoner be rescued? Will the poison be found before someone swallows it? Time, weather, adverse circumstances—not a human agency—are the agencies.

But that is another story. We are concerned here purely with the fear type of suspense situation, a most challenging and interesting form of mystery.

It is a good exercise for a writer to work out the minimum props you need to give your reader a genuine cold prickle. A man is standing in a phone booth on a deserted street; the phone starts to ring. This terrifies the man. Why? And how can it be made to terrify the reader, too? By what artful steps can one approach that phone booth so that the ring can seem an almost unbearable climax?

2

I COULD HAVE DIED LAUGHING

by *Robert Barnard*

BUT THERE'S NOTHING funny about murder!" It comes, occasionally, that shocked, conventional response to discovering that detective stories can be funny. Death has, in the eyes of many people, an aura of hushed reverence, and murder adds a dimension of horror. They would accept a melodramatic treatment, but not a comic one.

They are wrong, of course. Humor is one response to the human condition, and it must be allowed to operate on the whole range of experience that constitutes that condition. One does not need to go as far back as Scott or Dickens, both masters of gallows comedy. In our own day, Muriel Spark's oeuvre would be much the poorer without *Memento Mori,* her gruesome comedy of senility and death; and Fay Weldon's Olympian comic detachment enables her to deal with a succession of grisly disasters. The audiences who have laughed and shivered through Stephen Sondheim's *Sweeney Todd* are following a pattern set for generations: Their fathers and mothers flocked to *Arsenic and Old Lace,* and lugubrious comics in the British hall dealt with death with gloomy, chuckling relish. "More work for the undertaker," went one, giving a title to Margery Allingham's best detective story. . . . "another little job for the tombstone maker."

I think I fell into writing humorous crime fiction by accident. The first novel I wrote was serious. It was also predict-able and deadly dull. It concerned art treasures looted by the Nazis and hidden in Norway, and it was like every other book about art treasures looted by the Nazis. It was not, thank heavens, published. (How heartbreaking it is at the time, one's first rejection, but how heartwarming later!) But having a completed book under my belt, and a very encour-aging letter of rejection from one publisher who looked forward to seeing my next, I searched my mind for a sub-ject.

Apart from Norway, where I was then living, I had also spent five years in Australia. Australia is a lovely target—like a very large, slow-moving boxer, just waiting to be hit. Australians react with howls of pain to the slightest crit-icism, but—masochists all—they read the criticisms avidly. I had my subject and my potential audience. I would do a hatchet job on Australia.

From then on there was no doubt it would be humorous. In fact, during my time in Australia, I had been surrounded by very funny people. Funny-awful, mostly. I lined up my targets: the dusty, monotonous landscape; the dusty, mo-notonous people; the hopeless university; the pretensions of the graziers (ranchers I suppose you would call them). To this mixture I added a fat, lazy, stupid policeman (I was heavily influenced by Joyce Porter's *Dover One,* which I had recently read, and still think the funniest detective story I know). This was how my first novel *Death of an Old Goat* came about. The fact that it was accepted started me along that road (or got me into that rut, depending on your view-point). Most of my subsequent books have been, to a greater or lesser extent, of a humorous kind.

It never occurred to me that there was any problem about this. I was an admirer of Margery Allingham and Chris-tianna Brand, both of whom wrote books that were very funny, as well as being excellent detective stories in the elegant-artificial mode that I like best. Wit, characterization

with a touch of the Dickensian, caustic social comment—
none of these seems to me incompatible with the usual
procedures of murder and detection.

How much humor?

There are two dangers, though, one of them obvious, the
other less so. The first is that humor will hold up or swamp
the action, or detract from the essential interest of a crime
story: the body and the detection of its murderer. I find it
difficult to persevere in reading novels that are so high-
spirited that the murder itself is not taken seriously.
"Golly," the characters seem to be saying, "we're all having
so much fun that we can't actually worry about a little thing
like a corpse." I would not wish to cite a living writer here,
but some of Edmund Crispin's work may show what I mean.
And the René Clair film version of *And Then There Were
None* illustrates the dangers very clearly. It was all much
too jolly, and most of the characters gave not the slightest
feeling of being trapped on an island where one after another is being picked off in an unpleasant way. Exactly the
same is true of Christie on stage. If you try to send it up, the
results are leaden; if you play it for serious, it works. Yes,
the situation is artificial, unlikely, even bordering on the
absurd; but the contract between player and audience works
only if it is accepted as real and possible for the duration of
the play.

There is the lesson for the crime novelist. Murder is
serious to the people among whom it happens. All sorts of
fun and jollity may go on around it, but it must not be
treated as a negligible event by the characters remaining, or
the whole raison d'être of the crime novel disappears.

The second danger is the question of good taste. "It's
quite all right, provided it is dealt with in good taste,"
editors will say when confronted by a humorous tale of
murder. One is tempted to reply: "No, it is only all right if it
is dealt with in execrable taste." Ghastly good taste spells

the end of invention, surprise, and originality in fiction. But the crime writer can never entirely forget that he is writing for a mass market, and as a consequence he is obliged to insert his bad taste subterraneously, as a brief, sharp surprise, a grazing knife-blow through the ribs. Even then, some editor is likely to catch him out. But things do get past them: *Dover One* is a good example of what you can get away with in the matter of execrable taste.

I've mentioned Dickensian characterization. What I meant was broad, telling character creation that dwells in physical oddities and eccentricities of speech or behavior. One might cite the wonderful Palinode family in Allingham's *More Work for the Undertaker,* or the series character Lugg, Albert Campion's sidekick. Christianna Brand's detective Cockrill is similarly strongly etched, as are the inhabitants of her piratical Spanish-Italian island of San Juan in *Tour de Force*.

Quite often I have used monsters as victims: the Australian singer in *Death on the High C's,* or the mystery writer in *Unruly Son* (which in the States, alas, is called *Death of a Mystery Writer*). The latter figure was distantly inspired by the novelist Evelyn Waugh (whom I never met but admire more than any other modern writer), but I would never dare to use examples of social boorishness quite as dreadful as those actually committed by Waugh. That's the trouble with comic victims: They have to be toned down to be acceptable, and they leave an awful hole in the book when, round about page sixty, they are done in. More successful, I feel, was *Sheer Torture,* in which I used a whole family of elderly aristocratic artists and intellectuals. One of them is dead on the first page, but the rest are left to dodder and feud their way through the book, and this means there is no collapse of interest halfway through. It is my favorite book.

I mentioned toning down. The difference between Dickens's time and today is that now editors tend to shy away from the extraordinary or the grotesque; the jagged oddnesses of life pass them by, and they tend to prefer things smoothed into acceptable, unshocking shape. When my British editor said she found things in *Old Goat* that were exaggerated, I asked her to specify. All three of her examples were things that had actually happened or been said in the Australian university where I taught. So, granted this tendency to see life through smudged spectacles, in using comic characters we have to judge carefully how much we can get away with without being accused of going overboard. The fact that something actually happened cannot be used as a justification in itself: If the writer has not convinced the reader that it could happen, then he has quite simply failed. But we can, sometimes, use our characterizations to try to open readers' eyes. People can be much more awful, do things much more extraordinary, than Mr. Average is inclined to admit. Readers should be forced to see it, even if that means opening the door to nightmare.

The way they talk

The vital component of comic characterization is speech. The crime writer has less latitude than a Dickens, for the story has to move fast, and the reader resents any lingering as self-indulgence. A person's speech is a way of establishing briskly some elements of his character (conversely, the moment one feels the speech lying dead on the page, one knows the writer has not got that character properly in focus). Regional differences of speech are perhaps more marked in Britain than in the States, even today, and this is a help, but what the writer is primarily looking for is people who give themselves away in speech: the false exaggeration, the hypocritical protestation, the empty compliment.

I love writing dialogue, and I like it to move forward fast, so the crime novel suits me. I can hear Lil, the dreadful mother in *Mother's Boys* (*Death of a Perfect Mother* in the States—why do they do that to me?) shrieking her sexual innuendos in the pub; I can hear the Trethowan family mouthing their languid conversation barbs in *Sheer Torture*. Above all, I can hear the Conservative candidate and his mother talking on the phone in *Political Suicide*—my favorite piece of dialogue writing:

> "Mother?" said Anthony Craybourne-Fisk.
> "Yes? Who is it?"
> "You only have one child, Mother."
> "Oh, *An*thony," said Virginia Mavrocordatos, known to her friends and her wine-merchant as Ginny. "How *are* you?"
> "Fine. Mother, I'm standing."
> "You're what, dear?"
> "I'm standing for Parliament."
> "Oh, Par-li-a-ment. I thought . . . What on earth are you doing *that* for, darling?"
> "Well, it's the sort of thing one does."
> "Not *now*adays, darling. Nobody does. It's a positive hothouse of mediocrity. And the dress-sense of the members! Well, if you must, I suppose. It must be your father coming out in you."
> "I didn't know Father was political."
> "But of course he was, darling. Member for . . . that Midlands place, wherever it was."
> "That was Harold, Mother. Your second."

No firework display of wit, but I think an English person will *hear* the voices there.

I think most of the humor in my novels comes from character and speech, very little from action. An exception is *The Missing Brontë,* a dreadful book. To my mind, there are two problems with action. The first is that, in the age of film and television, *described* action comes a very poor second to *shown* action. I realize, from the popularity of thrillers, that few will agree with me. But I do not want to *read* about a man being chased across Iceland if I can *see* it. It is not as though the mental reactions of a man in that situation are likely to be complex or unpredictable. The same is true of comic action: It is not very funny to *read* about a man slipping on a banana skin.

The second problem is that, as the action gets fast and furious, the author, tapping away at his typewriter, is having a marvelous time, while the reader—well, all that visualization of described action does take it out of him. After a time he (or perhaps I should say I) tends to skip until things get less fast and hilarious. In other words, the danger of going overboard is particularly present when describing comic action. If, to get away with it, you require a reader in a particularly good mood, forget it. Readers are seldom so obliging.

In the end, it all comes down to having a comic eye, but exercising it with tact. Having the comic eye, most would think, is something that is bred into you or not, but I would disagree. I never remember finding things particularly funny when I was a child, and I find that as I grow older, comedy is becoming more and more of an effort, which may mean it is in danger of stopping being comedy at all. My last two books have been serious, and the best idea I have for the future is serious, too.

I don't regard this as an advance. Reviewers will say it is, as if comedy was the easiest thing in the world, but they will be wrong. Comedy is complex, profound, and difficult to keep up. I don't know whether my change of interest signals the access of a more melancholy temperament, or whether it constitutes intimations of mortality. But I do hope it's not permanent.

3

CHARACTERIZATION IN DETECTIVE FICTION

by *Rex Burns*

THE IMPORTANCE OF CHARACTERIZATION is second only to an author's having something to say. In detective fiction, especially with a series, it takes on added importance because the reader must be convinced that the protagonist is capable of the physical or intellectual demands of capturing a challenging villain. Let me first discuss my selection of a central character and then go on to the topic of presenting characters convincingly. What I say here will be primarily for detective stories, but much of it can apply to other narrative fictions as well.

The old saw about imagining your character in full before you start telling the yarn may be a good one, but I've seldom followed it. For one thing, I have trouble knowing everything about myself let alone about someone else, fictional or real. For another, I don't have the patience to complete a detailed biography before I start a story's action. What I do find indispensable to start with is a sense, often vague, of the protagonist's personality. With Gabe Wager, the hard-nosed homicide cop who is the central figure in my series, I wanted a character with intense personal pride—at times to a fault—and the kind of leathery toughness designated by the Spanish word "duro." That was his nucleus.

The physical details followed—some more quickly than others—and were chosen to support this personality: a

Spanish heritage (for the rigid pride) and short stature (for a bantam-rooster aggressiveness). He's also half-Chicano, half-Anglo. This was to heighten his isolation from both cultures and to emphasize the lone-wolf quality of his detection, a quality that so often puts him at odds with police bureaucracy. I'm not sure when I mixed his blood; it was before he had a name but after he had a soul, and somehow—given the soul—it seemed right that he be an "isolato." Gradually, but not until much later, I came to see him in much more physical detail: a small scar on his cheek, brown hair and eyes, sometimes a mustache. Usually, these characteristics would pop up as the story's development demanded. But the point is, these physical attributes (including his Spartan apartment and the Trans-Am he drives) are derived from his imagined core personality and from the requirements of the story's action rather than preceding them.

I followed the same process in creating Devlin Kirk, a central character I recently launched in a new series. But this time I was more aware of something I had only half perceived when I began with Gabe Wager: The personality must somehow be interesting. With Wager, that was an unexplored given; I was—and still am—fascinated by rigid personality surrounded by a fluid and at times chaotic world. But with Kirk, I actively searched my imagination for someone who could support a series of adventures and, one hopes, gather a following of readers. What would it take to provide such support? I'm embarrassed to admit how late in my writing career I discovered the simple answer: an intriguing personality. If the person interested me, I'd be more likely to hold the reader's attention.

Fundamental to this sustained interest is the question, "Will I be bored viewing the world through the protagonist's eyes?" If so, forget it; if not, go ahead and see what happens. The question has a lot of ramifications, entailing as it does the protagonist's quickness of eye, depth and agility of mind, and that ill-defined but vital thing called strength of character. Wager was primarily the result of a situation: What happens when a rigid figure tries to uphold the law in a world doing its best to be lawless. But that very rigidity narrowed considerably the spectrum of responses allowable. With Kirk, I purposefully chose a bright, well-read young man with a yearning for adventure and gave him just that quality. My hope, of course, is that throughout the series his mind will remain flexible so that I will not grow tired of seeing the world through his eyes. As with Wager, however, the nucleus of this protagonist wasn't physical appearance but a sense of his personality: quick-witted, self-confident, and daring, but with a strong element of reflective thought about the ultimate meaning of what he meets.

There's certainly nothing wrong in starting out with an image of a character's physical appearance—the only "rule" I've ever found in writing is "Do whatever works." But a protagonist usually requires some complexity of personality to sustain a reader's interest. Even with a severely one-dimensional protagonist such as James Bond, we can see Ian Fleming and, later, John Gardner offering more and more facets to his character, facets that have little to do with the tumultuous action that is the series' mainstay.

Another, and to my mind lesser, means of attracting readers to a character might—in contrast to the above—be called external. It tends to make use of props of some kind. One detective might, for example, grow orchids and be a gourmet chef; another might be a suave connoisseur of labels and brands. Whatever the prop, it serves to make the reader care about something out of the ordinary in the person, something that makes him stand out against the rest of humanity and thereby gives a cachet of expertise that heightens the probability of solving baffling crimes. With a central figure, however, the prop is often only a temporary eye-catcher, and the real appeal is found in the character's personality.

Portraying villains

The same external technique is often of help in quickly portraying villains and second figures. Think of the number of evil doers or sidekicks who are marked by an idiosyncratic quirk of behavior or a startling physical appearance. This verges on caricature, but there's no problem there; Dickens raised it to a high art, and a writer could do worse than to emulate his economy and clarity in presenting memorable figures. Indeed, in a story that's primarily adventure, there's often too little room for more than one "rounded" or complex character, and the yarn's rapid movement demands the economy of characters whose personalities can be summed up in a single phrase—"tough but kind," or "oily and cowardly." The trick, of course, is to present such characters so that they don't come across as clichés. How this is done exactly, I'm not sure. I try to find a balance between such a figure's central motif and his probable human behavior in the novel's various situations. Perhaps with more time on stage, this kind of person could grow into complex roundness—the potential is there. And perhaps that's what I'm trying to say: A convincing "flat" character is one who has the clear potential of becoming "round," but is not given the opportunity in the flow of the story.

The use of props for external definition of a character is obviously a means of presenting character. But I don't think it's the primary one. To my mind, voice is character. By that I mean the narrative voice that tells the story as well as the dialogue spoken by the characters. If a story's in first-person point of view, this primacy of voice is self-evident; the reader is addressed directly by someone ("I") who saw the action and is telling about it in his own words.

Like the direct address to the reader, internal monologue or stream-of-consciousness can also serve to establish or advance our sense of who a character is. My Gabe Wager yarns are told in the restricted third-person point of view so that the reader knows only what Wager knows, and when occasion demands, the reader can also know what's going on in his skull. Here's an excerpt from a longer passage in *Ground Money*; it's intended to give not only a glimpse of Denver, but also of Wager's detached and even sarcastic assessment of his home town, an attitude that tells us something about Wager's personality:

> . . . all over Denver Wager had seen a larger number of couples, many with children, setting up life in apartments and sharing houses with others. There was a touch of irony about that, for these were Anglos, the children of those who had taken their tax money out of the city to fill the surrounding suburbs with split-levels on lanes and drives and circles. Here their offspring were gradually developing the same kind of crowded and noisy neighborhoods Wager had grown up in. Now all they had to do was put in a corner grocery and a cantina and call it progress.

The clearest and often the most subtle means of presenting character is through dialogue between two or more speakers. In the following abbreviated passage from *Avenging Angel*, Wager and Axton are interviewing a man who discovered a body. I tried to let their voices reveal their states of mind as well as the orchestrated approach that Wager and Axton use on witnesses:

> "You guys believe me, don't you?"
> Wager looked at the witness. "Any reason we shouldn't?"
> "No! But . . . I mean . . . all the questions. . . . Honest to God, officer, I was just hitching along here!"
> Axton nodded. "We understand that, Mr. Garfield. We just want to get everything down now so we don't have to call you up later."
> Garfield sucked in a breath. "Yeah. It's just all of a sudden I thought, Jesus, what if you guys think I did it?"
> "We don't know who did it," Wager said. "Yet."

A worried and nervous witness, phlegmatic Max, and an abrasive and aggressive Gabe—these are the character traits I tried to let the dialogue reveal directly to the reader.

Note the lack of adverbs in the above swatch of dialogue. Wager doesn't say "grimly"; Axton doesn't speak "kindly"; the witness doesn't stutter "nervously." The diction and syntax of the dialogue, in conjunction with the situation of the speakers, will—I hope—carry the very sound of the voices, so that the extra baggage of instructing the reader how to read isn't necessary. In fact, it's a good exercise for writers to strike out the adverbs and see if the dialogue can stand on its own. If it can't, then, in most cases I would guess the writer doesn't have a clear sense of the voice—he doesn't hear the individual tones and word choices that make every person's language his own. And that's simply another way of saying he doesn't have a sense of his character.

Character change

In most fiction, character consistency is more effective than inconsistency, because the reader becomes oriented to a specific voice and behavior that have been given a name. But character consistency doesn't mean a lack of character change. For a long time, short fiction, especially, was built around the moment of character change; and many of the longer forms still trace a personality's journey from one condition to another. The so-called rounded characters are almost forced to undergo some kind of change because they're sensitive people who have faced some traumatic action. This is especially true in a series in which each volume is like a long chapter of an extended work. But the change in character generally should be consistent in order to be believable. This is another way of saying that, for me, character change comes from within and is based on the established personality. Sometimes, abrupt character change is explained as the result of an outside agent such as a demonic possession or chemical imbalance from a faulty experiment. But even in gothic or science fiction, the reader is offered some explanation to make that change plausible within the world of the novel. Post-modernist "experimental" fiction is a different game with different rules. There, character is usually made subordinate to theme by being reduced to comic or sardonic flatness, and often, the character's situation or predicament is more important than his psychology. In more traditional realistic fiction, such outside agents of radical change are generally unconvincing unless they're couched in terms recognizable in the real world which that fiction mirrors—head trauma, dope addiction, degenerative disease, etc.

Most often, a character's change is more slowly paced and has a quality of inevitability about it. I've found that once a character is clearly established in the mind, then the probability of that character's actions can be projected. The result is the kind of change and development I'm talking about. This is also the root cause of that delightful surprise when characters "take over" and the author seems to become less a creator than a reporter of what the characters tell him.

The characters in fiction come from the world around us and from within. What is it we're interested in about ourselves? What is it about neighbors and acquaintances that attracts us? What's the most fascinating personality we've met? Who would we like to be? What evil or despicable aspect of our lives or the lives of others intrigues us? Out of these and other questions come the nucleus of character and the character's own voice. But just as our lives are modulated by the restrictions of social behavior, so the lives of fictional characters are modulated by the demands of fictional structures. The characters in novels who loom in my mind are those who somehow find the right balance between the thrusting, vital energy of their lives and their roles as contributing figures in a narrative tapestry.

4

PLOTTING FOR MURDER
by *Max Byrd*

IN TRYING to explain to a correspondent why he wrote so
slowly—and with such stubborn, teeth-gnashing difficulty—
Raymond Chandler came up with an answer most aspiring
writers can understand:

> . . . it was always a plot difficulty that held me up. I simply would not
> plot far enough ahead. I'd write something I liked and then I would
> have a hell of a time making it fit in to the structure. This resulted in
> some rather startling oddities of construction, about which I care
> nothing, being fundamentally rather uninterested in plot.*

The irony, of course, is that Chandler chose to write detective novels, the most plot-dependent of all narratives. And like
every other detective writer, hard-boiled or classic, he had to
wrestle with the fact that the detective story is *self-conscious*
about plot. It calls attention to its own plot. At its conclusion,
the mystery story must not only announce a solution, but must
also review its whole earlier narrative in order to call attention
to its plausibility and logic. Anyone who sat through the
Agatha Christie movie *Evil Under the Sun* will have recognized in Hercule Poirot's interminable reconstruction of the
murder the classic device of summary and review that every
mystery requires. And anyone who tries to devise a mystery

*Raymond Chandler, *Selected Letters,* Frank MacShane, Editor (Columbia
University Press, N.Y., 1981), p. 81

27

plot will sympathize with Chandler's dilemma: In order to have the story come out right, you simply have to plot far ahead—you have to plot all the way to the end.

My first two Mike Haller mysteries (*California Thriller* and *Fly Away, Jill*) were written according to the trial-and-error procedure that Chandler describes. But when Bantam asked me to write a third Mike Haller novel, they gave me only a year to complete the typescript. Since I would be teaching a full academic schedule throughout that year, the necessity for plotting far enough ahead became urgent: I had not time in the schedule for trial and error or for massive rewritings.

First, I eliminated the stop-and-start process I had been using. I already had my case of detective characters—Haller, his partner, Fred, his friend Dinah—but I had no actual plot beyond the quite shadowy notion that I wondered what would happen if the clichéd threat actually came true: What would happen if Haller actually lost his license to be a detective?

After a solid week of staring at blank sheets of paper, I realized that I was not going to dream up a plot in a vacuum, certainly not a plot that would allow me to write quickly. The steps that I took next were helpful to me; perhaps other detective writers will also find something useful in them.

Plot categories

My first step was to make a catalogue of major detective plot categories that I recognized. I came up with seven:

1. *The caper*—perhaps the simplest of all plots, but in the right hands always a winner. This plot is basically serial: You know what the goal is—to rob a train (Michael Crichton's *The Great Train Robbery*), to assassinate someone (*The Day of the Jackal*)—and your plot consists chiefly of the preparations your protagonist makes. There is no need for reversals and surprises (until the end), for the plot is almost always a step-by-step account of assembling collaborators, scouting positions, introducing policemen, etc. Much of the enduring appeal of the caper plot comes from the same psychological source *Robinson Crusoe* first tapped: our vicarious

delight in planning and constructing elaborate schemes and structures.

2. *The ticking clock*—Nobody has done this better than Crichton in *The Andromeda Strain,* but almost every detective writer appreciates the built-in suspense of a deadline. Many writers have found the simple device of giving each chapter a date, place, and time of day makes a stubborn plot fall into place.

3. *Get me out of here*—The master of this is Peter O'Donnell, whose Modesty Blaise stories always have the same plot: the heroine is captured and imprisoned, and the British Cavalry come riding over the hill in the nick of time. (Donald Hamilton often uses this category in his Matt Helm novels.)

4. *The puzzle*—Agatha Christie territory. By her own account, she used to dream them up while doing the dishes. Perhaps it's because I can't think them up, but I agree with Chandler that there's no such thing as an honest detective puzzle. (I note in passing that the puzzle always stresses plot over character or style and is better adapted to comedy than to the realistic novel.)

5. *The Oedipal*—Ross Macdonald has made everyone aware of a fundamental principle of detective plots. There is always an *earlier crime.* This plot requires you to treat the present crime as a consequence of an earlier, perhaps forgotten one, and it requires you to push far back into the past to explain the present. A beautiful Chandler example, with no "oddities of construction" at all, is *The Long Goodbye.*

6. *Renaissance and Reformation*—the Pygmalion theme, in which an ordinary protagonist, mysteriously swept into crime or intrigue, is transformed into a stronger, harder, more dangerous person; or in which the hero remakes another person in his image. This works very well in spy and revenge stories such as leCarré's magnificent *The Little Drummer Girl,* where the girl "Charlie" is remade into a terrorist, and also in a psychological detective story like Robert Parker's *Early Autumn,* where the detective Spenser tutors a boy into manhood. Many of Simenon's Maigret detective novels revolve around the related mystery of a character who suddenly walks away from one life and takes up a new life and identity in another city.

7. *Reflective plots*—I thought of two examples at once: Dick Francis' *Whip Hand* . . . and *King Lear.* Here the subplots and the main mystery plot must converge in a resolution. Note that the first-person plot (the kind of narrative most beginning mystery writers should use, I think) requires that the subplot also concern the detective. In a third-person narrative, the subplot can employ different characters to reflect the various themes. To my mind this is by far the best of the plot categories because it relies upon the profound and commonplace truth that action arises from character.

Spinoffs

When I had studied this list I realized that any major plot category can be used as an element in another plot category. The caper plot can run according to a deadline—the ticking clock—and can, for example, conclude with a Modesty Blaise style escape. Any of the categories can be reduced to episodes or even scenes; and every kind of plot can employ reflecting subplots.

In plotting *Finders Weepers,* my third Mike Haller story, I found myself following three introductory steps that made use of what I had learned. For two weeks, I went back and forth each morning, doing and redoing in no special order one of these three things.

1. I wrote sketches of all my possible characters—biographies of one or two pages in which I described them physically, gave their ages, their schools, their quirks. Most of these had to be repeated several times, growing longer and longer; but when I came to the actual writing the sketches were invaluable and could often be used word-for-word.
2. I made a list of scenes. These were not plots but simply the kinds of things that could happen if Haller lost his license. He would be harassed by the police, for example, he would lose his license to carry a gun and would have to get one covertly (or do without!); in trying to regain his license he would threaten the criminal, who would therefore have to appear in the story at an early point to stop Haller's progress. I also thought of locations where scenes might take place. (Because small quantities of cyanide are often present in a greenhouse, I knew I wanted a scene to take place there. I also thought about chase scenes on boats in San Francisco Bay.) The order of all these scenes was completely random, but the simple presence of the list continually suggested other possibilities and additions.
3. I made a long summary—four or five typed pages—of the story that might develop. This was by far the hardest thing to do. The summary of the end was much thinner than the beginning, but it served as an extremely useful framework in which to start writing. I know some writers who make much longer summaries—fifteen or twenty pages or more—and they find the actual writing almost automatic, though of course every plot changes in some way as soon as you set it in motion.

Visualizing the end

Finally, I worked according to a principle that I had thought out myself, but that I subsequently discovered in John Braine's excellent book *Writing A Novel.* I tried to visualize the last scene in the story first. At its simplest level, after all, plot is no more than a mechanism for change. If you know what the end of your story looks like, you can far more easily picture what the beginning will have to be. But for me—and I think for many other writers—this last scene must be strongly visual. It is not enough to say that Mike Haller must of course regain his license. I had to *imagine,* in the strictest sense, what that scene would look like when it happened. The scene I imagined, in fact—long before title, setting, or even situation—was a fight in the surf, near the Seal Rocks on the edge of San Francisco Bay. I didn't know whom Mike was fighting, or why. But the physical setting was dramatic—I had seen it many times—and a battle in the water somehow suggested to my mind the psychological elements of frustration and release that Haller would have to go through in order to regain his license, that is to say, in order to regain his identity as a detective.

I had in mind another principle as well: the detective story, as I've said, ends by repeating itself. But I have long thought that *all* plots end by repeating themselves. Poirot does not repeat the story of the murder exactly as we saw it, however; he and all other detectives repeat the central episode in a new way. They give the unknown murderer a name, they call attention to a detail, they introduce an unexpected fact or motive. The plot, in other words, must remind us of what it has changed. We have to hear echoes of its beginning before we can understand that it is over. This is as true for *Great Expectations*—in which Dickens' famous second ending shows us Estella at last not rejecting Pip—as it is for *The Big Sleep,* in which Marlowe once again finds himself in Vivian Regan's bedroom sparring with her over the disappearance of Rusty

Regan, but this time telling her (and us) his version of the story with which we began in the famous opening chapters. Chandler may indeed have been uninterested in plot, but no writer, I suspect, can be uninterested in design.

5

WRITING MYSTERIES FOR CHILDREN

by *Mary Blount Christian*

WHENEVER I TALK to writers, the questions are the same: Where do you get the ideas for your stories? And how do you plot a mystery?

The quick answer is, everywhere and backward. The longer answer is only slightly more complicated.

Ideas are everywhere—on the newscasts, in the local newspapers, and even in the gentle art of eavesdropping at the mall and supermarket. I always carry a notebook and jot down the ideas I've heard. I have a shoebox filled with clippings—"rippings," to be more honest—from newspapers and magazines and even brochures.

Why a shoebox? Because I don't want to spend writing time trying to figure out whether to file a clipping under banks, burglaries, missing persons, etc. So I tear and toss. Whenever I need an idea, I shuffle through my stack until something grabs me emotionally. A piece on stolen bikes was only a curiosity when I collected it, but when two bikes were stolen from my family I felt a personal need to see a bit of justice done in an unjust world and wrote *The Goosehill Gang and The Bicycle Thief.* Perhaps another idea may arouse anger, regret, joy, or even hilarity. Somehow it must touch me emotionally before I can touch others.

As I rummage through my stack, I come upon clippings with the following headlines:

THREE CLOWNS WALTZ OFF WITH BANK MONEY
FIVE-YEAR-OLD WITH WALKIE-TALKIE SAVES ACCIDENT
   VICTIM
TOWN BRIDGE VANISHES DURING THE NIGHT
ELEPHANT MISSING FROM CIRCUS
WANTED: HOUSESITTER TO CARE FOR PETS, PLANTS
RETURNING VACATIONERS FIND EMPTY HOUSE
BULLDOZER FOUND CAB-DEEP IN GARBAGE DUMP
RASH OF BIKE THEFTS PUTS CHILL IN SUMMER

Collecting real-life situations is nothing new to writers. But beginning writers often fail to bring to the story their own personal experience to develop the idea into an orderly, meaningful situation. Editors have told me that at any given time they may have three stories on their desks all essentially alike, and all obviously based on an event that had received national coverage.

It will be that fourth story, where the original stimulus has vanished, that sells. Use the real-life situation only as a springboard to a more controllable idea, keep the limited capabilities of your young audience in mind, and be willing to do a bit of brainstorming. Then your story will become that fourth, irresistible story.

The leaves of a tree bear no resemblance to its roots, yet both leaves and roots are part of the same process. The nourishment from the roots is processed up through the trunk and recreated into something entirely different—the leaves. It is the same with a story. The writer becomes the trunk and reaches down into the roots to draw on that nourishment and transform it into a story—different, yet enjoyable.

Using and fusing ideas

My collection of ideas is extensive, and as I peruse it, some of the items will appear to relate to one another. A clipping about walkie-talkies setting off a burglar alarm and activating automatic garage doors relates to the clipping about the five-year-old hero and the walkie-talkie (which was the means of getting a kid not only into trouble but out of it). My personal contribution to the story was a recollection of my own childhood scrapes and my need to achieve and be respected by grownups. I saved only a few buzz words from that pair of clippings: walkie-talkie, automatic doors, and hero. All I needed to make the story develop was a likable, believable main character.

J. J. Leggett, Secret Agent, is a typical nine-year-old entertaining himself with his walkie-talkie until his mother, irritated at having the garage doors snap shut on her, sends him elsewhere to play. Next, he gets into trouble at the local bank when his walkie-talkie shuts the president inside the vault. Later, when he realizes that the bank is being robbed, he uses that same walkie-talkie to catch the thief. The final story had little in common with the real-life incidents.

When my mother-in-law called to say her stolen potted plants had been recovered and she had to go downtown to identify them, I visualized a police line-up consisting of green plants. Later, when my shoebox yielded that classified ad looking for someone to house-sit and care for pets and plants, I connected the two situations and created *The Green Thumb Thief.* In this book, my Undercover Kids are hired to plant-sit, and must recover the stolen plants before the owner returns. To add some humor, I had my child detectives use disguises, as I was fond of doing when I was young.

My son told me that his construction company was losing tractors, no matter what precautions were taken. Later on, I read that a county road grader had been half buried in a dump. I turned the combination of the two into *The Two-Ton Secret.*

Writers of children's mysteries should keep in mind certain basic facts: Youngsters are usually confined to their neighborhoods; depend on their bicycles for mobility and transportation; have limited physical strength; and are for the most part under the watchful eyes of adults, both at school and at home. The mysteries we write, therefore, must be believable and have a logical solution that one or more clever kids could work out within a limited time and space. Children have the advantage, however, of being considered by adults as ineffectual, so they often hear and see much more than adults suspect. These advantages, combined with the children's imagination and curiosity, help them solve puzzles and mysteries.

In a 32-page illustrated mystery with only 750 to 1,000 words, there is no room for false trails. I leave the physical descriptions to the illustrator's brushes and stick to the dialogue and action, which take care of most of the characterization. In 75 to 100 words, I introduce my main characters and the problem, and I use no more than that for the climax and wrap-up of loose ends, leaving the remainder for the development of clues. The children follow a trail of logic, and even when the clue doesn't give them the solution, it sends them to the next clue.

In *The Two-Ton Secret,* as Deke and Snitch search for a stolen bulldozer, they discover a two-inch layer of fresh earth on a dirt pile that has been there for several weeks. Maybe, they think, the bulldozer is buried there, but no. Still, that leads them to more fresh dirt behind the tool shed.

When the boys find no tracks outside the fenced-in area of supplies and equipment and no cut marks on the fence, they conclude that the bulldozer hasn't been stolen at all but is still on the property, or, more accurately, *under* the property behind the shed. The dirt displaced by the dozer has been added to the original pile of dirt, unnoticed by adults, who are looking for more obvious clues. The final clue is that the fence will be removed when the construction is completed. Deke summarizes that the thieves buried the dozer intending to dig it up once the fence has been removed, and then simply drive it away. What the children lack in sophisticated police equipment, they make up in logic and common sense.

The clues are all there; even if they don't understand them until the hero explains later, readers don't feel cheated. The hero can misread the clues, thereby misleading the reader, but it isn't fair to withhold something the viewpoint character knows.

The writer's commitment

Even though most of my ideas come from a situation or unique piece of information, they will not become stories until I have populated them and made a personal commitment to them. I look for a likeable hero, one like any other kid on the block, who gets into trouble at home, generally has a healthy appetite for food and adventure, and has a favorite playmate who is individual enough so the reader can tell them apart. And an important ingredient is humor, which can keep the adventure light and non-threatening.

I was approached by a publishing company to create four mysteries that could be solved by children using methods they have learned in first- through third-grade science projects. My first reaction was sheer panic. My science projects had always ended in mild explosions, holes in the carpet, or permanent spots on the ceiling. Still, the idea intrigued me. My personal commitment to this was a deep feeling that every child is unique and special and has worthy contributions to make in life. Before I even began to think about the mysteries I created a group of typical school kids with diverse ethnic backgrounds and talents.

Ann draws well and with her artist-viewpoint sees details that others may miss. Her twin, Walter, is a meticulous notetaker. David is an avid reader with interests in astronomy like his NASA-employed dad, and Pedro is a whiz with tools and creates needed instruments out of household items. The dog, Watson, has a good nose and canine curiosity, and his silly antics add welcome humor. Together they form the Sherlock Street Detectives.

Once I had my characters established, I went to an educational supply house and bought workbooks for Science I–III. Also, my editor sent me the science study guidelines and tables of contents from textbooks used throughout the country. If the solution is the flip-side of the problem, I reasoned, then wouldn't the problem be the flip-side of the solution? I *could* work backward. I'd find the solutions, i.e., the science projects, and then find a problem they could solve.

In *The North Pole Mystery,* for example, a compass plays a major part in the solution.

What does a compass tell me? Direction.

Why would I need to know direction? To know where to go.

Why am I going? To find something or someone. Something didn't work for me, because someone would have had to carry it there, and he'd remember where, wouldn't he? I decided on a small vulnerable someone. I added to my character list David's small brother, Adam, who was missing. Why would the compass be necessary to find a small boy? Because it had played a part in his being lost.

Why was a small boy interested in a compass? Because small boys are interested in everything. I had to be more specific. I decided that nothing interested little boys more than Santa Claus, and that meant the North Pole. So there I had my mystery and my solution. David is charged with watching his little brother but prefers to read his new book. When Adam pesters him to play Santa Claus, David distracts Adam with the compass, showing him how the needle always points north.

When Adam and the compass turn up missing, David and his friends realize that Adam is using the compass to find Santa at the North Pole, so they make a second compass, following it north to the treehouse, where they find Adam fast asleep. With that pattern in mind, I created three more stories, starting with the solutions—a weather vane, special knowledge about nocturnal animals, and satellites.

Chapter books

An optional format for young mystery fans, and one gaining popularity among publishers, is the "chapter book" or "stepping-up book." Each of these fills the needs of young fans who are good readers but unwilling to invest their time in full-length novels, and older children who either read poorly or who want a quick, entertaining read. Chapter books are also popular with teachers who read a chapter a day to their classes and find the books just right for one week.

When I have ideas that are more complicated than a 32-page book can handle, I use this chaptered format. I have two series—Sebastian (Super Sleuth), about an old English sheepdog that solves mysteries for his detective master, and the Determined Detectives, featuring Fenton P. Smith and Gerald Grubbs, with the unwanted help of Mae Donna Dockstadter.

These are 8,000 to 10,000 words divided into five to seven chapters with more suspects, more motivations, and more detailed subplots.

Whether you select the 32-page or chaptered format, you will need to give the main characters some personal stake in solving the mysteries. The Undercover Kids are trying to earn pocket change; Sebastian is saving the job of his detective master; the Determined Detectives have a knack for being in the wrong place at the wrong time; and the Sherlock Street Detectives are more aware of those most ordinary little mysteries that besiege us every day. Whatever the mystery, your characters must be likeable and believable, so that your readers will follow them with confidence, even down a shadowy alley, if necessary.

6 CLIMAX AND DENOUEMENT IN THE MYSTERY NOVEL

by *Stanley Ellin*

IN THAT EXCELLENT mystery novel *Jerusalem Inn* by Martha Grimes, a character, a literary gent, remarks about the mystery novel: "I've even tried to write one, but it's no good. . . . All those loose ends one has to tie up. . . ."

All those loose ends, indeed.

And it's axiomatic that the more elaborate the plot of the novel, the more loose ends there will be to tie up and all the more wordage will be required for a proper tying-up.

> "You see," said the Great Detective, "when Mrs. Lafarge proved she had taken the 9:04 train I was badly stumped. Then I realized that if she had slipped off the train at Utterings, bicycled to the Old Manse (that would explain those oil stains on her Adidas) . . . ."

Recognize that? It is a cooked-up sample of denouement, that wind-down of the story following its climax where the detective now explains his mental processes in solving the crime. A little of this goes a long way. Several tightly packed pages of it can dampen the effect of the entire novel. Up to and including the climax the story was powered by the dramatic interplay of its characters. Now, in its denouement, it becomes a tableau, a stageful of waxworks placed in position to hear out the Great Detective. Of course we want his explanation, but must it be delivered as a sort of gray expository afterword to the high drama that preceded it?

Before answering, let me turn to the dictionary:

> *climax*: (In a dramatic or literary work) a decisive moment that is of maximum intensity or is a major turning point in the plot.
> *denouement*: The final resolution of the intricacies of the plot, as of a drama or novel.

Thus the climax in our sample story is reached when the Great Detective aims a finger at Mrs. Lafarge and grimly says—to the astonishment of his auditors—"There is the killer!" whereupon Mrs. Lafarge either whips out a pistol but is readily disarmed (the Great Detective has been prepared for this move), or heads for the nearest door where she runs into the arms of the waiting police, or breaks down and blubbers a confession.

End of climax, and, as Mrs. Lafarge is led away, opening of denouement. The effect can be as troublesome as if one saw a movie in full color up to its climax, whereupon it abruptly shifted to black and white for its denouement.

Playing fair with readers

Yet, the final explanations of the detective's mental workings are necessary. While I've learned in over forty years of toiling in the vineyard that most pat rules about writing the mystery novel were made to be broken, the one that stands unchallengeable is that the writer play absolutely fair with the reader. No rabbits up the sleeve, no invoking the supernatural. Cold logic must finally prevail, but—and this is the important point—it should be introduced without cooling off the heated drama preceding it.

The solution to this can be found in characterization, by which I mean depth of characterization. If your story is pure puzzler—an extremely tricky plot presented through two-dimensional characters tailored exclusively to this purpose—there is almost no escape from the need to end up with a lengthy and undramatic denouement. But if your major characters—and most notably the protagonist doing the detection—are plausible human beings, you have the means to end the narrative on a high note, one that will leave the reader moved as well as enlightened.

In the initial draft of my first novel, *The Eighth Circle,* in which I introduced a professional private investigator, the plot was extremely complex, and the P. I. himself was simply a hired hand paid to untangle it. And, willy-nilly, at the conclusion of the story when he had completed the untangling, there he was delivering a tedious lecture on his deductive processes, the very thing that has set my own teeth on edge in reading some otherwise entertaining classic puzzlers.

When the light finally dawned—and let's not go into how many typed pages hit the wastebasket along the way—my protagonist, still the consummate, well-paid professional, had a powerful stake in the case, the woman he had come to love, and he also had a moral issue to work out within himself: the self-destructive cynicism bred in him by his vocation and the warped view this gave him of the people he dealt with. So the denouement did not merely consist of his describing his deductions but of a bitter self-realization, culminating in the decision to give up that vocation.

In *The Key To Nicholas Street,* I created a protagonist driven to solve a murder out of love for a woman whose family is deeply involved in it. At the climax, he does identify the killer, the son of the family, but now in the denouement, having come to understand and pity the boy, he—along with the family—faces the crucial question: Which of them will turn the boy over to the police? And with all of them gathered together in torment, it is the resolution of that question that sustains the dramatic level of the story's climax through its denouement.

In *Mirror, Mirror On the Wall,* admittedly a pretty horrific psychosexual case study, the climax came naturally with the identification of the killer, but along the way, consciously or otherwise, I had focused on the protagonist's growing need to learn not only *who* had committed the crime but, almost as urgent, *why* it was committed at this particular time and place. The answer to the first question provided the climax of the narrative; the answer to the second helped maintain dramatic tension to the last line of the denouement.

Maintaining dramatic tension

The forgoing examples suggest that there are two elements that can help a mystery novel maintain dramatic tension to its final words. First, whatever the motive that draws the protagonist-detective into a case, he must develop an emotional tie to that case, through moral righteousness or compelling love for someone in its orbit or a justified vengefulness or any such valid attribute of his nature. Whether he is a hardened professional investigator or a wide-eyed amateur, identifying the perpetrator will not be enough for him; there must be more to it than that.

Second, the denouement, essentially the process of reasoning, no matter how dramatic, should be as tightly compressed as possible. This does not mean reduction to synoptic form, but it does mean that of all places in the novel in which the writer must beware of falling under the spell of his own beautiful prose, this is it. Remember that the story has peaked at its climax—that's what makes it a climax—so that no matter how effectively dramatic tension is sustained through the denouement, it is still at a lower level than the climax.

7

METHOD FOR MURDER
by *Loren D. Estleman*

OF ALL FICTION, the detective story has tended most often to reflect the sophistication of its readers. This explains why a mainstream classic like Joseph Conrad's *Lord Jim* remains as fresh today as when it appeared in 1900, while the first Ellery Queen adventure, *The Roman Hat Mystery,* published nearly thirty years later, is all but unreadable.

The distinction has little to do with quality, as some of the western world's finest writers spent their careers breaking down alibis and tracing buttons clenched in victims' fists. Rather, constant exposure to the mystery form, whether directly or by osmosis, has taught the average reader most of the tricks of diversion that were daring and new in Queen's time but rob the story of its mystery in this more worldly era.

Thinking like your detective

Increasingly, the detective-story writer has to come to rely upon story value over gimmickry in his incessant attempt to hold his audience. Just as life itself has grown more complicated with time, so must the plot of the mystery, and with it the need to occupy the reader with a story intriguing enough on its own to keep his attention through its many detours and 180-degree turns. And in order for the writer himself not to become lost, he will do well to think like his detective.

I'm often asked if the Machiavellian nature of my mysteries

requires a more detailed outline than the average fictional plot. It surprises people to learn that I never outline and seldom know where my story is going when I start writing. As a result, I often find myself desperately treading water during the writing process to avoid drowning in the high tide of unresolved situations, implausible coincidences, and inadequate motivations. When this happens, I simply take a deep breath and throw my arms around my detective, trusting him to lead us both to shore. Once I ask myself how Detroit private eye Amos Walker would react to this or that development, I'm as good as rescued.

Example: Two-thirds of the way through *The Glass Highway,* my fourth Amos Walker mystery, I came to a shrieking halt when all of Walker's leads dried up and it appeared that he and I would never learn what became of the mystery woman for whom he's searching. Like a detective, I went back over the facts, flipping through the early manuscript pages until I found this soliloquy of Walker's, delivered to that same woman:

> ". . . The city prosecutor runs the town, and he's a crook. The police department has several hundred thousand federal revenue-sharing dollars tied up in enough electronic flash to remake *Star Wars,* but what the cops get the most use out of is their twelve-volt cattle prods. Any Saturday night you can ring three longs and two shorts on some rich resident's doorbell and be shown into the basement where a dogfight is going on. There's a former city attorney named Stillson on the main drag who specializes in probate work, but if you're a friend of a friend and have twenty thousand to spare he'll make you the proud parent of a brand-new black-market baby. If you're hot, he'll sell you a complete new set of identification for a grand. . . ."

As originally drafted, the speech was intended only to provide color on a corrupt suburban community and help delineate Walker's mildly crusading character. But now I realized that he had inadvertently supplied the woman with a means of escape through the information about the attorney who sells false identification papers. When Walker remembered this, it gave him a new handle on the case that eventually led to its solution—and me to a bang-up conclusion for the book.

Call it luck or the subconscious at work, I am continually inserting such carpenter's eyes for no reason that I can fathom other than that they seem to lend more depth to the story, only to come up a hundred pages later with just the hook that will fit into one of them. I should add, however, that I wind up removing a number of those that continue to flap loose from the final draft, something I would probably not have to do if I outlined the project first. The decision whether to blueprint a book beforehand or let it grow naturally is the writer's own and should depend on the amount of control he can bring to a work in progress.

Playing fair with the reader

To sharpen the pivotal point in *The Glass Highway,* I was obliged to go back to that early soliloquy and give the crooked attorney a name, something he didn't have previously, so that the woman could be expected to have made contact with him later. It's necessary to plant such seeds early on to avoid having too many convenient explanations flying out of left field during the inevitable expository sequence at the climax. In mystery parlance, this is called playing fair, giving the reader a chance to solve the puzzle with the facts at hand, but in the larger fictional sense it has to do with plausibility. All the labor you put into making your detective a believable character will come to nothing if you allow him to make a string of brilliant deductions in a short space of time without substantiation. If, as is the ideal, the reader has failed to anticipate your solution, he should be able to look up from the page and say, "Sure, why didn't I think of that?"

Perversely, this makes the detective-story writer's job more difficult, for now he must insure against making his mystery too transparent. At this point, a follower of the classic English school would drag the well-known red herring—a phony suspect or a false clue—across the path to divert the reader. But because the device is so well known, it is no longer enough. It thus becomes the writer's chore to take it one step further and create an entire new subplot to pull over the thin place, concealing it and drawing attention away from it. This practice is by no means new—Dashiell Hammett invented the whole business of the search for the Maltese Falcon more than fifty years ago expressly to prevent his readers from looking too closely into the murder of Miles Archer—but it's still effective when handled skillfully, and carries the extra advantage of making the story more interesting and realistic. Any police officer will attest to the fact that real-life mysteries are often obscured by such peripheral matters.

There will come a time, too, when your murderer seems too obvious. When this happens, don't panic. Approach the problem head on and have your detective either consider and reject the character as a suspect until more evidence is in, or just number him among the others and let the reader make of the facts what he will. It's O.K. if he suspects the truth. The writer's only obligation is to provide choices. Do not make the mistake of fitting the crime to the least likely suspect, as readers have long since been aware of that chestnut and will automatically consider the "least likely" the culprit.

How many clues

Never underestimate the detective-story fan's capacity for pleasure in correctly identifying the murderer, or for hostility when he fails. One reviewer grumpily accused me of chicanery in *The Midnight Man* for exposing one of its more likable characters as a murderer. But I had set out all the clues fairly; he was just out of sorts because he'd missed them. Still, the tightrope between giving away too much and not giving away enough should be trod carefully. The reader might often be abreast of the detective, sometimes behind, but he must never, never be ahead, or respect is forfeit.

The writer who has avoided making his mystery too easy runs the danger of making it too complex, losing the reader among the red-herring subplots, tangled motives, and enigmatic characters. This is not as disastrous as it could be, as long as he has succeeded in placing story value ahead of whodunit. But some sort of lifeline should be provided to pull the reader to safety. At such times, I like to remember the way Felix the Cat used to stop the action midway through his cartoons, turn toward the viewer, and say something like, "Boy, am I in trouble. The Master Cylinder has me trapped. . . ," thus bringing late arrivals up to date. Without being so blatant, the detective might at this point freshen faulty memories through dialogue or introspection. After a significant development in the plot of *Motor City Blue,* I had Walker light up one of his ubiquitous Winstons and muse:

> The Kramer burn was related to the Shanks killing, which was related somehow to Marla Bernstein's/Martha Burns' disappearance. If Beryl Garnet was telling the truth, her description of the man who bankrolled Marla's room and board in the cathouse on John R fit Freeman Shanks as well as it fit a thousand other guys. That explained the attempt to disguise himself during his visits, which was unnecessary if the old lady never watched television or read a newspaper as she claimed, but he wouldn't have known that. . . .

And so on. It's plausible as well as helpful, since your detective is human and can be expected to have to arrange his impressions from time to time in order to keep them clear in his own mind. The average reader has as much trouble identifying with genius as has the average writer.

Unraveling the plot

Mysteries that fail usually do so in their closing pages. This is the place where, no matter how scrupulously you have planned your surprises, the detective and the other main characters must unravel the more knotty details of the plot through dialogue. This can be tedious at the one point where it's crucial not to be. Some kind of tension is necessary to hold the reader's interest while all this talking and explaining is going on. Someone must be holding a gun or someone must be inching toward a lamp cord. Suspense must be maintained. This expository scene from *Angel Eyes* speaks for itself:

> "Find that gun," he told the towhead, jerking his chin in the direction of the Cadillac.
>
> Tim grumbled something about just having gotten his suit back from the cleaners, holstered his .45, and got down on his hands and knees to peer under the car. I moved back a step.
>
> "He had a stroke." Clendenan was watching the tableau in the doorway. "Not five minutes after he burst in looking for Mother. He collapsed, and when he finally came to, it was obvious that his brain was affected. Sometimes he's lucid. The rest of the time he's like a ten-year-old. . . ."
>
> "It isn't under there." Tim climbed to his feet and dusted off the knees of his trousers.
>
> "Look on the other side," said the secretary.
>
> While he was watching the bodyguard circle the car I slipped the revolver into the side pocket of my jacket and left it there with my hand around it. . . .

By switching its emphasis back and forth between competing acts as in a two-ring circus, the scene builds anticipation while imparting necessary data. Without the promise of some kind of fireworks at the end, the unfolding of the mystery can be about as riveting as a monotonic reading of the Dead Sea Scrolls.

As the detective story continues evolving to meet the ever-shifting interests of a developing culture, the rules governing its structure must change as well. But the writer who wishes to reach his public cannot go wrong by remembering that he is telling a story first and creating a mystery second. By placing himself in the role of his detective, planting seeds, juggling subplots, and respecting reality, while catering to his audience's love of challenge, he will solve the always intriguing problem of how to attract readers. Which in the end is really the most important mystery of all.

8

BREAKING AND ENTERING
by *Sue Grafton*

SEVERAL YEARS AGO, a long-suppressed desire to write a detective novel began to work its way into my consciousness. I had long been attracted to the genre, spending many a satisfying evening immersed in the intricate puzzles of fictional homicide. As a detective fiction reader, I was experienced; as a writer, I knew absolutely nothing about private investigation, police procedure, forensics, criminal law, or suspense and mystery techniques. Writing novels had taught me how to create character. Writing film and television scripts had taught me dialogue, but plotting was not my strong suit. There I was, a big fan of Agatha Christie, Ross MacDonald, Raymond Chandler, Elmore Leonard, Lawrence Block, Dick Francis, et al. The very idea of competing with such craftsmen scared me half to death. I couldn't think of a better reason to jump in.

Intuitively, I knew that writing detective fiction, like Chinese cooking, would require a lot of advance preparation. I began to do research—the single most important step in the writing of any manuscript. I sorted through my back issues of *The Writer,* culling articles on mystery and suspense writing. I consulted various texts on mystery and suspense fiction and added Lawrence Block's *Writing the Novel: From Plot to Print* to my home library.

A search through the public library catalogue revealed a number of books about private investigation. To begin with, I read three: *Handbook of Criminal Investigation,* by

Maurice Fitzgerald (Arco); *The Investigator,* by James Ackroyd (Frederick Muller Ltd.); and *Technics* (sic) *for the Crime Investigator,* by William Dienstein (Charles C. Thomas). Once I settled on a southern California setting for my projected novel, I acquired *California Criminal Law, California Criminal Procedure,* and *The California Evidence Code.* I did additional reading from a local medical school library on the subjects of forensic pathology and toxicology.

"Creating" your detective

Having armed myself with a broad range of general knowledge, I then sat down to decide what kind of detective novel I wanted to try. In the course of my reading, I had isolated three basic types: the police procedural, in which a homicide detective working for a city or county police department undertakes the solution to a murder case; the "private eye" novel, in which a private investigator or insurance adjuster pursues a suspicious death; and a third category, in which an amateur investigates a murder, tracking down the true culprit to clear his or her own name or to protect the reputation of someone else. I felt no particular affinity for the amateur detective, and since I didn't have the skills or the inside knowledge to tackle a police procedural, I was left with option number two, the licensed private detective. Because I felt more comfortable writing from a woman's point of view, I made my detective female. I chose Santa Barbara as my setting (renaming it Santa Teresa in the book) because I had lived there for six years, and was far enough away at that point to distill my own memories into a fictional California locale. My personal recollections were shored up with street maps, travel guides, picture books of southern California and promotional literature published by a Santa Barbara press. Perhaps unwittingly. I was practicing the first piece of advice that most writers are given anyway! Write about something you know. The detective genre was new to me and challenge enough in itself. After that, I needed the comfort of the familiar to see me through.

Even before I had fashioned a plot, I wrote an opening to see if I could capture the right tone. I tried first person, self-conscious about the echoes from Raymond Chandler and James M. Cain, convinced that I would never find my own "voice" in the midst of theirs. I wrote about two pages, sounding somehow like a shady character trying to palm off a hot watch. Just to demonstrate, I'll include here the original quote. "My name is Kinsey Millhone. I'm what they call a 'dick,' though the term is something of a misnomer in my case. I'm a woman . . . a female adult. Maybe you know the kind. I'm also a private investigator. I'm 36, married twice, no kids. I'm not very tough, but I'm thorough. . . ." This piece of silliness sat on my desk for a year. At intervals, I would try again, generally in the same hard-boiled mocking Mae West accent. At one point in the writing, still without plot, I had Kinsey Millhone called on the telephone by a man who identified himself as John D-O-U-G-H. I knew that I could never sustain an entire book in this manner. Furthermore, I had no desire to do so. I wanted to write a "real" detective novel, not a *spoof* of one. It's clear to me now that because I felt ill-at-ease with the form, my own discomfort was getting in my way, rather like a telephone line being jammed by static. The interference, in my case, was raw anxiety.

I turned my attention to the story itself and decided to worry about tone some other time. I began to play "Suppose . . ." and "What if. . . ," trying premise after premise with characters designated simply as X and Y. Suppose X wants to murder Y and the scheme misfires so that Z is killed instead. . . . What if Z kills X? T figures out that Z is guilty. T tries to kill Z but misses, killing Y instead. Two murders. Same M.O. Second murder is revenge for the first. As I played with ideas, the notes became less sketchy! High blood pressure medication. Off on business trip. Violent symptoms . . . nausea, vomiting, cramps. D.O.A. What assumption would be made? Food poisoning? What kinds of poison can be traced? What is the procedure? Urine? Blood tests? How long does it take? The development of the story progressed as I filled in these blanks.

By bombarding myself with questions over a period of time, I found that some lines of inquiry were more persistent than others, some more appealing. A few popped up so often that a tale began to take shape, the questions becoming statements instead. "A prominent Santa Teresa divorce attorney dies one night after taking an allergy capsule laced with oleander. His wife, accused of the murder, is convicted and serves eight years in the California Institute for Women, hiring Kinsey Millhone when she gets out on parole to find the person who really murdered him." X and Y became characters with real names and individual identities.

I set up a biographical file for each character that came to mind, again plying myself with questions, this time pertaining to personality and motive: What kind of person was Laurence Fife? Why did so many people hate him? I adopted various personae, telling the same story from different points of view until I understood each character's relationship to the book as a whole. Some characters were invented, and some I fleshed out from people I knew, borrowing traits and mannerisms until a character sparked to life independently.

The outline

By now, two years had passed, and the story was like a crossword puzzle with most of the answers filled in. Finally, with a rough sketch plot laid out and the main characters defined, I began to construct an outline, detailing scenes as I felt they should occur. Along with the step outline, I drew up a "plot map" with the characters' lives laid out in chart form, indicating births, deaths, marriages, divorces, affairs.

1961 Laurence Fife (b. 1934) opens own law firm

1962 Mrs. N.'s suicide

1963 Sharon goes to work for Laurence; Charlie Scorsoni joins Laurence's firm

1964

1965 Charles S. made a partner in Laurence's firm

1966

1967 Gwen's affair

1968 Gwen and Laurence divorce

Many such events were outside the actual time frame of the novel, but they were facts I needed to know, and the "plot map" allowed me easy visual access to complex character histories. In conjunction with the "plot map," I devised a "sequence of events map" in which I determined the order in which events came to pass. Again, this was helpful in keeping tabs on the narrative which stretched back many years. These incidents happened within months of the murder of Laurence Fife and were directly connected to his death.

1973 June	July

Nikki out of town; Colin at the beach house

August	September

Family vacation 8-31 through 9-3; Diane sick; dog killed

October	

Rx filled 10-5; Laurence dies 10-8; Libby calls Scorsoni 10-9, when she hears the news

All of these events were essential to the plot, though the book itself opens eight years later, when Nikki Fife gets out of prison and gets in touch with Kinsey Millhone. As with any other outline, scenes were added, deleted or ignored as the developing story dictated. Not every character would agree to say lines of dialogue I had penned in advance. Not every point worked as planned. Still, the maps and charts gave me the tangible evidence I needed that I did know what I was talking about and where I meant to go.

Throughout this stage, I continued to amass work sheets in which I challenged every aspect of the project from the smallest detail to the overall point of view. What is the thrust of this book? The point is that truth and justice are not the same thing. In the end, when the whole case finally comes together, and Kinsey understands the events, someone gets killed, and someone else gets away with something. And that's just the way the world is these days. Kinsey will never quite make sense out of it, but life itself isn't sensible. Nothing is tidy and that has to be all right since none of us has a choice anyway.

As I took myself more seriously, the tone I had been searching for began to come through clearly. I realized that I saw the detective novel as a serious examination of contemporary issues. I started the book again at page one, and oddly enough, the actual openings of *"A" Is for Alibi* is not that far from my first glimmerings. The tone by then had been molded and refined. I had found a "voice" that I felt comfortable with—my own.

"My name is Kinsey Millhone. I'm a private investigator licensed by the State of California. I'm thirty-two years old, twice divorced, no kids. The day before yesterday, I killed someone, and the fact weighs heavily on my mind. . . ."

9

SEEING AROUND CURVES
by *Martha Grimes*

SOMETIMES I WONDER if painters and potters are asked, "How far along are you?" with that portrait or vase, or "How much have you done?" with that landscape or bowl. Such well-intentioned inquiries into the progress of a novel make me feel a little cross and, in a way, slightly stupid, as if I, naïve traveler on the Orient Express, were asked to describe the Venetian canals before my feet had left the platform in Victoria.

People seem to grasp the idea that a painter does not see an orange or an ear floating in his mind's eye, and a potter does not see a neck or a handle. But perhaps because we all "write" in some sense, there is a certain familiarity about pages, and they think progress can be charted by counting them. Perhaps paintings and pots are seen spatially, as a whole, but stories and novels are seen as linear. An eye doesn't "follow" an ear in a portrait, but it's a dead cert that page two will follow page one in a book. And because of this, when I say "a hundred and fifty pages," my interrogator might answer, "Ah. Halfway through, then." No, definitely not, I tell him, no more than I'd have painted half a face if I had got down the eye and the ear.

But if one sees writing in this way—as linear—it is understandable that one might be more likely to look at it as a trip, with marked distances to go between colorful chapter stop-offs. And the mystery writer especially may lean toward this idea of inventing a sort of Triptik or map or other means of charting the territory he intends to cover, then peopling it with characters, and drenching it with atmosphere. Since it is true that in a mystery there should be no loose ends and no clues unaccounted for, it is likely that one might think all story plot problems are resolved in good time.

Character directs the journey

This assumption that the emphasis in the mystery novel is on eventful happenings or crises—like the murder itself, for it is most often murder—sometimes obscures the fact that the ax doesn't hang in the air, but must be dropped by someone's hands on someone's head. It also assumes that we who write it must know about Venice before we leave Victoria Station. Yet few people know exactly what their destination will look like before they get there or even if they will reach it. So we don't know where we are until we see what it looks like, and we don't know who we are until we see what we do. No one can see around curves no matter how far he sticks his neck out the window. Plot—the territory we want to chart—depends on the characters as much in a mystery as it does in any other novel; character directs the whole journey.

Many writers apparently do very well by mapping out the trip before they start, by sorting out what we might think of as the central elements of plot in a mystery—the perpetrator, the victim, the means, and the motive—and getting them into place by means of outlines, summaries, and synopses. On the other hand, there are writers who just go ahead and climb aboard the train, uncertain even of their destination, perhaps taking their chances that some unknown factor will keep the train from derailing.

I suppose I work this way because I find it so difficult to untangle plot from character, to invent crises for strangers.

Nor do I think the device of the character sketch written ahead helpful, because what Tony had for tea when he was seven doesn't interest me unless at twenty-seven he's going to lace someone else's tea with cyanide. Plot, character, setting all seem one huge tangled skein when we set out to write. And because it's difficult to untangle the elements, you might think that the Grand Design should be set down before you have characters bumping into one another on the platform. Line them up and make them behave, for heaven's sakes! There goes the Colonel, making for the café. *Thwack!*

Now let's say that the sketches, the outlines, the synopses, or the plot summaries are all approaches that you feel will at least get you aboard the Orient Express. You take your character-sketched people along and thus you and Sybil and Grimthorpe and the Colonel manage to get into the dining car (oddly lacking in ambiance since you would hardly have included that in your plot synopsis). The four of you are having a good gossip and being quite friendly, all of you with copies of the outline/sketch/synopsis before you.

You're all in a pretty good mood, except when the Colonel becomes rather churlish because he can't get the waiter's attention. Of course he can't because there is no waiter; he was not in the Triptik.

Now, Symbil, Grimthorpe and the Colonel read over the outline/sketch/synopsis. And there the trouble begins. Fortunately, the dining car is unpeopled—since the background passengers weren't in the synopsis—and the four of you can have a high old time:

Sybil is furious because you're having her marry Grimthorpe when the Orient Express hits Venice. Sybil claims she wants to marry Anthony.

Who's Anthony, you wonder? watching her dampen her finger and plaster a spit-curl to her cheek as she gazes out at the empty (truly empty) countryside.

"Sybil," you ask patiently, "*why* must you marry Anthony?"

"Well, *I* dunno, do I?" Then she rolls her eyes and adds, "I s'pose because he's ever so 'andsome. . . ." She swings her leg and twirls a cheap sequined bag. . . .

But Sybil's supposed to be a marchioness. Why is she coming on like a shopgirl?

Grimthorpe's mouth twiches as he looks down his knobby nose at Sybil and announces he wouldn't have her on a bet.

The Colonel's face is beet-red because he can't find a waiter, yell as he might.

You now realize something's wrong and wonder how the devil you're going to get out of this mess as the Orient Express chugs along to Paris. The only thing you're sure of is that they'll all detrain in Venice—

Until the train rolls into Paris, and Sybil just gets off. Anthony lives in Paris. . . .

The reader is certainly familiar with what is practically a cliché—that after a while the "characters simply take over." This is actually one of those wonderful remissions (or reprieves) for the writer, when everything seems to be on automatic pilot, and the people in your book "come alive," and appear to know what they're going to do and how they're going to do it. You would be willing to believe that the Muse indeed visiteth at such times. The Muse or Tinkerbell or Inspiration or something. But since you know that characters do not clear the mental compartments and take over themselves, it must be some other part of your mind doing it, and all of the scenario above is probably the unconscious ditching the lovely plot complications of the conscious mind. In other words, Sybil (part of you) has a reason for tuning out all of that highbrow marchioness stuff; you simply don't know what it is, any more than you can see around curves. But you will eventually know why, and eventually round the curve. That you will either go mad at worst or type away in a state of controlled hysteria (at best) is something writers like me have to put up with if they want to get to Venice.

From "notion" to novel

All of this revolves pretty obviously around another question that makes me cross: "Where do you get your ideas?" *Idea* is a word that seems frighteningly all-encompassing and makes me think of Carl Sagan neatening up the cosmos. *Idea* really does sound as if the interrogator is asking you where you got your *plot*. And the whole point is—how on earth do you know what people are going to do (correction, what you're going to *have* them do) until you see what they've done so far?

Perhaps I'd opt for the word (if there must be one) of "notion." That sounds far more frivolous, something rather small and capable of being grasped. It could be *anything*. The "notion" for *The Man with a Load of Mischief* came purely from the name of a pub. That a pub would have such a strange name led me on the further notion that a mystery set in England and having something to do with pub names might be interesting. My original detective was an effete, snobbish aristocrat, whose only saving grace was the wit of Oscar Wilde. Unfortunately, I had to toss that one out, since I don't have the wit of Oscar Wilde. Anyway, this character ultimately became Melrose Plant, and by that time, Scotland Yard had insinuated itself into the mystery in the person of Richard Jury. Perhaps the reason I am so fond of British pub names is that the germ of an idea can be found in so many of them. *The Anodyne Necklace* was irresistible for this reason. The notion of someone's killing for a necklace with curative powers was all I climbed aboard with.

The initial "notion" might be anything concrete—scene, sound, smell. I think if you confuse "notion" with "theme," you are definitely on the wrong platform, and you'll be sitting on your suitcases forever. *Theme* is an abstraction; it is not a cause but an effect.

The notion for my novel *The Old Fox Deceiv'd* was nothing more than a mental image of a youngish woman walking along a dark and cobbled street. In this case, it was a setting that attracted me, and memories of the quintessential English fishing village called Robin Hood's Bay that I had visited ten years before. I was writing this plotless book when in one day I saw, in three different places, a woman dressed in black and white. It was Halloween, and one of them, in a black cape, was walking across a low-rising hillside. The three became a composite that begins the story:

> She came out of the fog, her face painted half-white, half-black, walking down Grape Lane. It was early January and the sea-roke drove in from the east, turning the cobbled street into a smoky tunnel that curved down to the water. . . . The wind billowed her black cape, which settled again round her ankles in an eddying wave. She wore a white satin shirt and white satin trousers stuffed into high-heeled black boots. The click of the heels on the wet stones was the only sound except for the dry *gah-gah* of the gulls.

Here, it was setting and atmosphere that intrigued me. I liked the idea of a young woman walking along the pavement of an English fishing village, and that someone be waiting in either a door- or alleyway, and that a knife come slashing down. I had no idea (1) who the girl was, (2) why she was being murdered, (3) who was murdering her. When I wrote the opening quoted above, the only additional thing I knew was that the young woman was either going to or returning from a costume party. That made me think of the various "disguises" and the endless possibilities arising therefrom for murder and mayhem.

I have probably used about every banal convention of the British novel of detection I can think of (hoping, of course, nothing appears to be banal in the end) simply because I like them. Bodies dumped in snow, letters dipped in vitriol, corpses stuffed in trunks. I have not actually used the near-holy device of the train schedule for some reason, but I imagine it will come up at some point.

When I sit down to write a book the only thing I'm sure of is that I'm there at the moment. Talent isn't guaranteed, but discipline is at least dependable, like any other habit. Fortunately, it's more productive than smoking and drinking. Flannery O'Connor said that although she might not come up with an idea for the allotted time she was there, at least she was there in case one happened along.

I have been asked (sometimes accusingly) why in the world I, an American, would set her books in England. Like Sybil, "I dunno." Probably I was on my way to Venice and got off, by some quirk, in Little Grousdean, where I sat around in the local pub with Sybil and Grimthorpe and the Colonel, arguing over train schedules and drinking Old Peculier.

10 TOPICS AND TENSIONS IN MYSTERY WRITING

by *Jeremiah Healy*

I HAD BEEN A LAWYER for only five years when I began teaching law school. My practical experience having been limited pretty much to the courtroom, I felt a little presumptuous in thinking that at thirty I was capable of being a professor. By the end of my first year of teaching, however, I realized that I could provide something of value to the students; I was still close enough to the beginning of my law career to remember—and warn against—the hazards a novice lawyer would face.

My mystery writing career is somewhat parallel: In the few years since I began writing mystery—particularly private detective—novels, I have encountered many difficulties, and with luck, I will be able here to offer the same kind of caveats for novice mystery writers that I was able to offer my law students.

I'll discuss these caveats in the form of "topics and tensions."

Structure: discipline vs. freedom

There are a number of established mystery writers who prefer not to use outlines. For someone starting out, however, I think the key to writing effectively (meaning salably) is having a good plot, and I think the key to a good plot is a good outline. I start thinking about a story the same way I used to conceptualize a lawsuit—by deciding where I want to be at the end of the case and backtracking from there. At the end of a lawsuit, I want the jury to come back in my client's favor. For that to happen, I have to present, in some coherent form, a sequence of events through witnesses and documents that will persuade the judge that the jury should get to decide the case. That means I have to backtrack conceptually from where the case will end to where it began (the intersection accident, the signing of the contract, whatever), recognizing along the way which people, places, and events I will need and want (there is a difference) to include.

I believe that it is best to structure a mystery novel the same way: Decide on your ending, then backtrack to decide who and what you include where, so that the story, run forward, will make sense and be entertaining. The beauty of this system is that your "backwards" outline forces you to think through each essential element of the puzzle in its logical place, so that you then can vary its position as deflection and masking of your mystery require. That same process also will save you substantial time overall, as you will be wasting less effort creating well-wrought scenes that just don't "fit" your story. Also, if you have to squeeze your writing in around full-time job or family commitments, the backtracked, elaborate outline, once completed, allows you to write the story forward in little segments, which will tend to be consistent with each other even though actually written some days or weeks apart. I know that some writers believe that excessive outlining stultifies the imagination. I believe that a certain amount of imposed discipline allows one to have the freedom to create within that discipline.

Length: expansion vs. padding

You ought to have some idea of the length requirements of the markets to which you're aiming your work. If on doing an approximate word count you come up short, ask yourself if you can somehow expand the plot, perhaps by adding a character whom your detective could talk with in an additional scene. Don't pad your work with descriptions of sunsets or irrelevant wise-guy repartee.

Content: exposition vs. action

A reader will tolerate only so much exposition about a character's personality or philosophy. It is better to demonstrate that trait implicitly by action. If you want your character to be violent, don't describe her as such. Instead have her hit someone. If you want your character to be sarcastic, have him say something sarcastic. To paraphrase Hemingway, if you as the writer talk too much about a quality, you will lose it.

Dialogue: identification vs. flow

When a viewer watches a movie, there is no question which character is speaking: It is the actor whose lips are moving when the words are heard. In a short story or novel, however, there is a need to identify the speaker in order for the reader to understand the scene. Some writers overreact, identifying every character each time he or she utters a word. This tends to inhibit the flow of the story and to frustrate the reader.

One way to avoid this tendency is to restrict each scene to no more than two characters. Robert B. Parker is a master of this device. He allows the reader to identify the speaker merely by the break in the paragraph of dialogue, with only occasional "she said" and "I said" signposts to give the reader who suffers a lapse in concentration a cue back into the flow of dialogue.

Another approach is to have each character in a scene speak distinctively, in a slang or accent. Avoid, however, excessively phonetic cuteness, especially when associated with ethnicity or race. It can be offensive to some readers and tiresome to all. Read Elmore Leonard to see how one can capture, for example, black street language without stooping to elaborate caricatures of pronunciation.

Lastly, I believe dialogue flow is harmed by the use of verbs other than the word "said." Do not have your characters "murmuring," "gasping," or "chortling" their lines. The words they speak, rather than your choice of expressive verb or adverb, should convey the impression you wish to create.

Physical description: memorable vs. comprehensive

We all want the reader to be able to visualize the character we see so vividly in our mind's eye. The trick, though, is to realize that the reader, especially of a novel, will have a hard time remembering from chapter to chapter all the physical characteristics you've described in such detail. I suggest, therefore, that you try to focus on one striking characteristic or mannerism for each character, if possible one that reflects his or her personality or is integral to his or her role or action in the story. A bad guy with terrible body odor is memorable if you highlight that aspect of him. You might have the hero realize the bad guy is lurking around the corner by being able to smell him before seeing him. To distinguish another character, you can borrow a celebrity's familiar image, as "a blocky, middle-aged man who bore an uncanny resemblance to Spencer Tracy." However, the reader rightly will think you lazy if you resort to this shorthand more than once in any given story or novel.

Inhumanity: violence vs. revenge

I believe you have to tailor, if not curtail, the amount of inhumanity you attribute to your characters and the world they populate. Revenge is a strong and believable motivation, but violence *per se* should be used judiciously and only to advance the storyline. Probably most people, if polled, say there is too much violence in our society. If pressed with the right questions, however, I suspect that most would say there is too much of the *wrong kind* of violence and not enough of the right kind. Put simply, your reader will be troubled by the punk who slaps an elderly woman across the face, cutting her cheek with his ring. The same reader will be reassured by seeing your hero break that punk's nose in a gesture of speedy justice—so long as the retribution, though more severe than the crime, is not grossly disproportionate to it.

Motivation: apparent vs. real

A common piece of advice to fledgling trial lawyers is never to try to sell the jury something you wouldn't buy. In writing, this is especially true regarding character motivation. In writing a mystery, you must show that the motivation for your culprit's actions is necessary for the advancement and resolution of your plot. To do this generally requires you to develop two motivations: the *apparent* motivation and the *real* motivation.

The apparent motivation is the reason for an action that masks the real motivation, revealing your character as the culprit. The apparent motivation can be relatively flimsy; indeed, it is often its flimsiness that encourages your hero to investigate further. The real motivation, however, must be basic, strong, and credible: revenge, power, money, sex, blackmail, or the avoidance of scandal involving one or more of these. If you don't believe that the culprit's real motivation is strong enough, don't expect an editor or a reader to, either.

Authenticity: imaginary vs. real

Authenticity is important if, forgive the circularity, you need to be authentic. Crime writer Ed McBain can create streets in the prototypical but fictional city depicted in his 87th Precinct series, but Robert Randisi has to have the right subway lines running to the right destinations in his books about Manhattan and Brooklyn. Both of them, however, make sure their characters don't try to drive an Edsel made in 1968 or fire a Smith & Wesson Chief's Special revolver that has seven bullets in the cylinder. If you must include a subject that you don't already know well, you must first research that subject, and then have an expert check the parts of your manuscript that deal with it.

I hope this advice will help some of you avoid pitfalls by spotting them before creating them. I think the only way you really improve your performance in writing mysteries is by practice. If you want to become a better trial lawyer, you try more cases. If you want to become a better writer, you write more stories.

11 BUILDING WITHOUT BLUEPRINTS
by *Tony Hillerman*

IN 37 YEARS OF WRITING, I have accumulated two bits of wisdom, that may be worth passing along.

First, I no longer waste two months perfecting that first chapter before getting on with the book. No matter how carefully you have the project planned, first chapters tend to demand rewriting. Things happen. New ideas suggest themselves, new possibilities intrude. Slow to catch on, I collected a manila folder full of perfect, polished, exactly right, pear-shaped first chapters before I learned this lesson. Their only flaw is that they don't fit the book I finally wrote. The only book they will ever fit will be one entitled *Perfect First Chapters*, which would be hard to sell. Thus Hillerman's First Law: NEVER POLISH THE FIRST CHAPTER UNTIL THE LAST CHAPTER IS WRITTEN.

The second law takes longer to explain. When I defend it, I'm like the fellow with his right arm amputated arguing in favor of left-handed bowling. However, here it is:

SOME PEOPLE, SOMETIMES, CAN WRITE A MYSTERY NOVEL WITHOUT AN OUTLINE.

Or, put more honestly: If you lack the patience (or brains) to outline the plot, maybe you can grope your way through it anyway, and sometimes it's for the best.

I was in the third chapter of a book entitled *Listening Woman* when this truth dawned. Here's how it happened:

I had tried to outline three previous mystery novels. Failing, and feeling guilt-ridden and inadequate, I finally finished each of them by trying to outline a chapter or two ahead as I wrote. I had tried for weeks to blueprint this fourth book, sketching my way through about six chapters. At that point, things became impossibly hazy. So I decided to write the section I had blueprinted. Maybe then I could see my way through the rest of it.

I wrote the first chapter exactly as planned, an elaborate look at the villain outsmarting a team of FBI agents on a rainy night in Washington, D.C. I still feel that this chapter may be the best 5,000 words I've ever written. By the time I had finished it, I had a much better feeling for this key character, and for the plot in which he was involved. Unfortunately, this allowed me to see that I was starting the book too early in the chronology of the story I was telling. So this great first chapter went into the manila folder (to be cannibalized later for flashback material). Then I planned a new opening. This one takes place now on the Navajo Reservation at the hogan of an elderly and ailing Navajo widower named Tso. It is mostly a dialogue between him and a shaman he has summoned to determine the cause of his illness. The chapter was intended to establish time, mood, and the extreme isolation of the area of the Navajo Reservation where the novel takes place. It would give the reader a look at Tso, who will be the murder victim, and introduce the shaman, who would be a fairly important character. Finally, the dialogue would provide background information and—in its discussion of Navajo taboos violated by Tso— provide clues meaningless to the FBI, but significant to my Navajo Sherlock Holmes. Again, all went well, but as I wrote it I could sense a flaw.

It was dull. In fact, it was *awfully dull.*

I had planned to have the second chapter take place a month later. In the interim, Tso has been murdered offstage, and the killing is an old unsolved homicide. Why not, I wondered then, have the murder take place during the opening scene? Because then either (a) the shaman would see it, tell the cops, and my novel becomes a short story; or (b) the murderer would zap the shaman, too, messing up my plot. At this stage, a writer who specializes in Navajos and has accumulated a headful of Navajo information searches the memory banks for help. Navajos have a terribly high rate of glaucoma and resulting blindness. Why not a blind old woman shaman? Then how does she get to the isolated Tso hogan? Create a niece, an intern-shaman, who drives the old lady around. The niece gets killed, and now you have a double murder done while the blind woman is away at a quiet place having her trance. You also have an opportunity to close the chapter with a dandy little non-dull scene in which the blind woman, calling angrily for her newly deceased niece, taps her way with her cane across the scene of carnage. The outline is bent, but still recognizable.

Early in chapter two, another bend. The revised plan still calls for introducing my protagonist, Navajo Police Lt. Joe Leaphorn, and the villain. Joe stops Gruesome George for speeding, whereupon G.G. tries to run over Joe, roars away, abandons his car and eludes pursuit. Two paragraphs into this chapter, it became apparent that Joe needed someone in the patrol car with him to convert the draggy internal monologue I was writing into snappy dialogue. So I invent a young sheep thief, handcuff him securely, and stick him in the front seat. He turns out to be wittier than I had expected, which distorts things a bit, but nothing serious goes wrong. Not yet. Leaphorn stops the speeder and is walking toward the speeder's car. As many writers do, I imagine myself into scenes—seeing, hearing, smelling everything I am describing.

What does Leaphorn see? His patrol car emergency light flashing red reflections off the speeder's windshield. Through the windshield, he sees the gold rimmed glasses I'll use as a label for Gruesome George until we get him identified. What else? My imagination turns whimsical. Why not put in another pair of eyes? Might need another character later. Why not put them in an unorthodox place—peering out of the back seat of the sedan? But why would anyone be sitting in the back? Make it a dog. A huge dog. In a crate. So the dog goes in. I can always take him out.

Still we seem to have only a minor deflection from the unfinished, modified version of the partial outline. But a page or two later, in chapter three, it became obvious that this unplanned, unoutlined dog was going to be critically important. I could see how this ugly animal could give the villain a previous life and the sort of character I had to hang on him. More important, I could begin to see Dog (already evolved into a trained attack dog) could be used to build tension in the story. As I thought about the dog, I began to see how my unblueprinted sheep thief would become the way to solve another plot problem.

Since that third chapter of my fourth mystery novel, I have honestly faced the reality. For me, working up a detailed outline simply isn't a good idea. I should have learned that much earlier.

For example, in my first effort at mystery fiction, *The Blessing Way,* I introduce the Gruesome George character in a trading post on the Reservation. He is buying groceries while my protagonist watches, slightly bored. I, too, am slightly bored. So is the reader. Something needs to be done to generate a bit of interest. I decide to insert a minor mystery. I have the fellow buy a hat, put his expensive silver concha hatband on it, and tell the storekeeper that someone had stolen the original hat. Why would someone steal a hat and leave behind an expensive silver hatband? My protagonist ponders this oddity and can't think of any reason. Neither can I. If I can't think of one later, out will come the hat purchase and in will go some other trick to jar the reader out of his nap. But the hat stayed in. My imagination worked on it in the context of both the Navajo culture and my plot requirements. It occurred to me that such a hat, stained with its wearer's sweat, would serve as the symbolic "scalp" required at a Navajo ceremonial (an Enemy Way) to cure witchcraft victims and to kill witches. When my policeman sees the stolen hat (identified by the missing hatband) in this ritual role, it leads him to the solution of his mystery. (And the author to the completion of his book.)

Creative thinking

I have gradually learned that this sort of creative thinking happens for me only when I am at very close quarters with what I am writing—only when I am in the scene, in the mind of the viewpoint character, experiencing the chapter and sharing the thinking of the people in it. From the abstract distance of an outline, with the characters no more than names, nothing seems real to me. At this distance, the details that make a plot come to life always elude me.

Another example: In *Fly on the Wall*, the principal character is a political reporter. He has been lured into the dark and empty state capitol building in the wee hours on the promise that doors will be left unlocked to give him access to confidential tax files. He spots the trap and flees, pursued by two armed men. Before I began writing this section, I had no luck at all coming up with an idea of how I could allow him to escape without straining reader suspension of disbelief. Now, inside these spooky, echoing halls, I think as my frightened character would think, inspired by his terror. No place to hide in the empty hallways. Get out of them. Try a door. Locked, of course. All office doors would be locked. Almost all. How about the janitor's supply room which the night watchman uses as his office? That door is open. Hide there. (Don't forget to dispose of the watchman.) A moment of safety, but only a moment until the hunters think of this place. Here are the fuse boxes that keep the hall lights burning. Cut off the power. Darken the building. Meanwhile, the readers are wondering, what's happened to the night watchman? Where is he? That breathing you suddenly hear over the pounding of your own heart, not a yard away in the pitch blackness, is the watchman, knocked on the head and tied up. Check his holster. Empty, of course. So what do you do? The hunters know where the fuse boxes are. They are closing in. Feel around in the darkness for a weapon. And what do you feel on the shelves in the janitor's storeroom? All sorts of stuff, including a gallon jug of liquid detergent. You open the door and slip out into the dark hallway, running down the cold marble floor in your sock feet, hearing the shout of your pursuer, dribbling the detergent out of the jug behind you as you spring down the stairs.

In an outline I would never have thought of the janitor's supply room, nor of the jug of liquid detergent. Yet the detergent makes the hero's escape plausible and is a credible way to eliminate one of the two pursuers as required by the plot. Even better, it is raw material for a deliciously hideous scene—hero running sock-footed down the marble stairway, liquid soap gushing out behind him from the jug. Bad guy in his leather-soled shoes sprinting after him. Except for describing the resulting noises, the writer can leave it to the reader's imagination.

A big plus for working without an outline, right? The big negative is that I forgot Hero had removed his shoes and had no way to recover them. The editor didn't notice it either, but countless readers did—upbraiding me for having the hero operating in his socks throughout the following chapter.

How will it come out?

I have learned, slowly, that outlining a plot in advance is neither possible, nor useful, for me. I can get a novel written to my satisfaction only by using a much freer form and having faith that—given a few simple ingredients—my imagination will come up with the necessary answers.

Those ingredients—not in any order of importance:
- *A setting with which I am intimately familiar.* Although I have been nosing around the Navajo Reservation and its borderlands for more than 30 years, I still revisit the landscape I am using before I start a new book—and often visit it again while I am writing it. And then I work with a detailed, large-scale map beside my word processor.
- *A general idea of the nature of the mystery* that needs to be solved, and a good idea of the motive for the crime, or crimes.
- *A theme.* For example, *The Dark Wind* exposes my Navajo cop to a crime motivated by revenge—to which Navajos attach no value and find difficult to understand.
- *One or two important characters,* in addition to the policeman-protagonist. However, even these characters tend to be foggy at first. In *Dance Hall of the Dead*, the young anthropology graduate student I had earmarked as the murderer turned out to be too much of a weakling for the job. Another fellow took on the role.

When I finish this, I will return to Chapter Eight of the present "work in progress." My policeman has just gone to the Farmington jail, where I had intended to have him interview a suspect. Instead he has met the suspect's attorney—a hard-nosed young woman who, as the dialogue progressed, outsmarted my cop at every turn. This woman did not exist in my nebulous plans for this book and has no role. But I have a very strong feeling that she will assume one and that it will be a better book because of her.

That's a good argument against outlines. Without one, I can hardly wait to see how this book will turn out.

12

ONE CLUE AT A TIME
by *P. D. James*

FOR ME one of the keenest pleasures of rereading my favorite mysteries is their power to transport me instantly into a familiar world of people, places and objects, a world in which I feel at once comfortably at home.

With what mixture of excitement, anticipation and reassurance we enter that old brownstone in Manhattan, that gentle spinster's cottage in St. Mary Mead (never fully described by Agatha Christie but so well imagined), that bachelor flat in London's Piccadilly where Bunter deferentially pours the vintage port [for Lord Peter Wimsey], that cozy Victorian sitting room on Baker Street.

A sense of place, creating as it does that vivid illusion of reality, is a necessary tool of any successful novelist. But it is particularly important to the fabricator of the mystery: the setting of the crime and the use of commonplace objects help to heighten by contrast the intruding horror of murder. The bizarre and the terrifying are rooted in comforting reality, making murder more believable.

There is probably no room in crime fiction that we enter with a keener sense of instant recognition than that claustrophobic upstairs sitting room at 221B Baker Street. Baker Street is now one of the dullest of London's main thoroughfares, and it is difficult, walking these wide pavements, to picture those foggy Victorian evenings with the inevitable veiled lady alighting from her hansom cab outside the door of the celebrated Sherlock Holmes.

But we can see every detail of the room into which Mrs. Hudson will usher her: the sofa on which Holmes reclines during his periods of meditation; the violin case propped against the wall; the shelves of scrapbooks; the bullet marks in the wall; the two broad windows overlooking the street; the twin armchairs on each side of the fireplace; the bottle of 7-percent-cocaine solution on the mantel shelf; the desk with the locked drawer containing Holmes's confidential records; the central table with "its white cloth and glimmer of china and metal" waiting for Mrs. Hudson to clear away.

The mental scene has, of course, been reinforced countless times in films and on television, but what is remarkable is that so vivid a picture should be produced by so few actual facts. Paradoxically, I can find no passage in the books that describes the room at length and in detail. Instead, Sir Arthur Conan Doyle builds up the scene through a series of stories object by object, and the complete picture is one that the reader himself creates and furnishes in his own imagination from this accumulation of small details.

Description, mood, and suspense

Few things reveal the essential self more surely than the rooms in which we live, the objects with which we choose to surround ourselves, the books we place on our shelves, all those small household goods that help reaffirm identity and provide comfort and a sense of security. But the description in crime fiction of domestic interiors, furnishings and possessions does more than denote character; it creates mood and atmosphere, enhances suspense and is often crucial to the plot.

In Agatha Christie, for example, we can be confident that almost any domestic article mentioned, however commonplace, will provide a clue, either true or false. A loose door number hanging on its nail; flowers that have died because no one watered them; an extra coffee spoon in a saucer; a picture postcard lying casually on a desk. In *Funerals Are Fatal,* we do well to note the bouquet of wax flowers on the malachite table. In *Murder at the Vicarage,* we can be sure that the tall stand with a plant pot standing in front of the window isn't there for nothing.

And in *The Murder of Roger Ackroyd,* we shouldn't be so intrigued by the corpse that we fail to notice how one chair has been strangely pulled out from its place by the wall.

All writers of mystery fiction use such devices, but few with such deceptive cunning. It is one of the paradoxes of the genre that it deals with that great absolute, death, yet deploys the trivia of ordinary life as the frail but powerful instruments of justice.

Because in a Christie mystery the puzzle is more important than either the characterization or the setting, she seldom describes a room in great detail. Hers is the art of the literary conjurer. How very different is the loving care and meticulous eye with which a novelist such as Margery Allingham creates for us her highly individual domestic interiors.

In *More Work for the Undertaker,* how brilliantly she describes every room of the eccentric Palinode family, so that the house itself is central to the plot, its atmosphere pervades the novel, and we feel that we know every secret and sinister corner.

But my favorite Allingham rooms are in *The Tiger in the Smoke,* with its opposing characters of the saintly Canon Avril and the psychopathic killer Jack Havoc. How simply described and how absolutely right is the Canon's sitting room. "It was the room he had brought his bride to 30 years before, and since then . . . nothing in it had ever been changed. It had become a little worn in the interim, but the good things in it, the walnut bookcase with the ivory chessmen displayed, the bureau with 13 panes in each glass door, the Queen Anne chair with the 7-foot back, the Persian rug which had been a wedding present from his younger sister, Mr. Campion's mother, had all mellowed just as he had with care and use and quiet living."

Right, too, in its very different style, is the sitting room of his dress-designer daughter, Meg, littered with its sketches of dresses and strewn with swaths of material and samples of braids and beads. "Between the damasked grey walls and the deep gold carpet there ranged every permissible tint and texture from bronze velvet to scarlet linen, pinpointed and enlivened with daring touches of Bristol blue."

This is a highly individual room in the grand manner but without pretentiousness, and I'm not in the least surprised that after a dubious sidelong glance, Chief Inspector Luke decided that he liked it very much indeed.

A room I like very much indeed is Lord Peter Wimsey's sitting room in his flat at 110A Piccadilly. We see it most clearly through the eyes of Miss Murchison in Dorothy L. Sayers's *Strong Poison*. She is shown by Bunter into a glowing, book-lined room "with fine prints on the walls, an Aubusson carpet, a grand piano, a vast chesterfield and a number of deep, cozy armchairs upholstered in brown leather.

"The curtains were drawn, a wood fire blazed on the hearth, and before it stood a table with a silver tea service whose lovely lines were a delight to the eye." No wonder Miss Murchison was impressed.

After his marriage, of course, Lord Peter honeymooned with his Harriet at Talboys, an Elizabethan farmhouse in Hertfordshire that Lord Peter bought as their country retreat, complete with inglenooked fireplace, ancient beams, tall Elizabethan chimneys, erratic plumbing and the inevitable corpse in the cellar. Meanwhile, the dowager Duchess of Denver was busying herself collecting the chandeliers and tapestries for the Wimseys' town house in Audley Square and congratulating herself that the bride "was ready to prefer 18th-century elegance to chromium tubes." I am myself partial to

18th-century elegance, but I still feel more at home in that bachelor flat at 110A Piccadilly.

Incidently, Talboys was modernized and completely refurnished, including the installation of electricity and the provision of additional bedrooms, before the murderer of its previous owner had been executed—in England a matter then of only a couple of months. That was remarkably speedy even for the 1930's. Today I am doubtful whether even the son of a Duke would be able to command such speedy service.

The ordinary made terrible

I work in the tradition of Margery Allingham and share her fascination with architecture and domestic interiors; indeed, it is often the setting rather than a particular character or a new method of murder that sparks my creative imagination and gives rise to a novel.

In my book, *The Skull Beneath the Skin,* the setting is a restored Victorian castle on a lonely, offshore island. Here the owner, obsessed with violent death, has created his own private chamber of horrors, a study decorated with old woodcuts of execution scenes, Staffordshire figures of Victorian murderers, mourning regalia and the artifacts of murder.

Here I have used the setting to fulfill all the functions of place in detective fiction: to illustrate character, create atmosphere, provide the physical clues to the crime and to enhance that sense of unease, of the familiar and ordinary made strange and terrible, which is at the heart of detective fiction.

And it is surely the power to create this sense of place and to make it as real to the reader as is his own living room—and then to people it with characters who are suffering men and women, not stereotypes to be knocked down like dummies in the final chapter—that gives any mystery writer the claim to be regarded as a serious novelist.

13

HAVE YOU TRIED MURDER?
by *Peter Lovesey*

Dear Mr. Lovesey,
> I understand that you are a writer of murders. I think you will be interested to know that I have thought of a totally new and original form of murder that I am sure you could use in a book. It is simple and quite undetectable; in fact, the perfect murder. I guarantee that it will work. May I suggest that we meet for lunch in London at some mutually convenient time and place, when I am confident that we can agree on a suitable fee?
>
> Yours in crime,
> s/A.D.Z_____

When I get letters like this, I feel bound to wonder at the profession I pursue. What makes anyone into a mystery writer? An aggressive personality that needs channelling into something not too dangerous? An unhealthy interest in the macabre? Or just the hope of becoming rich and famous?

Dear Mr. Z_____,
> Thank you for your offer to sell me a perfect murder. Unhappily it is of no use to me because I deal exclusively in murders that are imperfect. Otherwise the detective would never solve the crime. I am sure there must be people who would be glad to buy your idea, but if you have a conscience you will keep it to yourself.
>
> Yours sincerely,
> s/Peter Lovesey

There's a story about an old lady standing by the bookstall on a London railway station. She had been there a long time, looking more and more depressed.

81

A sympathetic assistant asked, "Can I help you?"

The old lady said, "I can't find anything suitable to read on the train."

"Yes," said the girl. "It's nothing but Agatha Christie—rows and rows of horrible murders."

"I know, dear," said the old lady. "I wrote them."

Dear Mr. Lovesey,
I have just watched your television play *Waxwork,* in which the victim was poisoned with cyanide used in his photographic studio. I like nothing better than an old-fashioned murder mystery, especially a poisoning. By a strange coincidence my husband Harry's hobby is photography, but I am not sure if he uses cyanide. I had a look in the darkroom, but I couldn't see any. I wouldn't ask Harry in case he gets the wrong idea. He is an ignorant man who doesn't understand the woman's point of view, but that's another story. On another matter entirely, could you settle an argument by telling me how much cyanide is needed for a fatal dose, and if it can be detected in hot chocolate?
s/(Mrs.) Jane S——
P.S. The reason is that I am writing a book.

The letters are not all so disturbing. I tell myself that the serious murderer is unlikely to betray his plans to a mystery writer. But even letters like this, which I suspect are written in fun, remind me that mine is a rather dubious area of literature. Graham Young, one of Britain's most notorious poisoners in recent years, kept a diary in which his victims' names were listed, and he claimed in his defense that they were notes for a novel he was working on.

Soon after my first mystery was published, I was invited to join a club for mystery writers. A weekend conference was announced. The agenda was formidable: a police chief on the hunt for a vicious multi-murderer; a forensic expert with a talk entitled "Every Contact Leaves its Traces"; a visit to the local police headquarters; and finally, a slide show by a Home Office pathologist. I went along out of curiosity, but in trepidation at the prospect of meeting people well-versed in ballistics, poisoning, and signs of strangulation.

I learned a lot in that weekend. The most valuable thing I

learned was not on the agenda: that mystery writers are in general inoffensive, genial, and disarming. Those I met—they included several famous and best-selling authors—admitted to some unease at being lectured on the grim realities of crime. One well-known writer of at least a dozen murder mysteries told me he would have to miss the slide show because he fainted at the sight of blood. (Several other seats were conspicuously vacant.)

When I got home, I reflected on it all. If mystery writers were reluctant to be brought face to face with death and violence, what were their books about? Was mystery fiction still as remote from harsh reality as it had been in the so-called Golden Age of Agatha Christie, Dorothy L. Sayers, and Margery Allingham?

> A drawing room, or is it a library, crowded with suspects.
> An inscrutable butler with a plateful of freshly baked scones, of the most appetizing appearance.
> "Won't you try one?" enquired Sir Jasper.
> The Inspector returned an enigmatical smile. "I have lost my appetite."
> "Oh, hell!" said Jasper forcibly. He glanced quickly to his left.
> "Watch out, Sergeant—the French windows!" snapped the Inspector.

Without detriment to the craft and ingenuity of the Golden Age writers, it is clear that the best mysteries of today are more crisply written and sharper in their observation. They are better researched, less mealy-mouthed in their accounts of violence, and more realistic in their dialogue. Yet Agatha Christie still dominates the bookstands, and Sayers, Allingham, and Ngaio Marsh still sell like the hot cakes endlessly eaten in their drawing rooms. What, I asked myself, is the secret of the enduring appeal of mysteries that established their style over half a century ago?

A game as well as a story

The first and obvious conclusion is, that like no other form of fiction, the true mystery novel presents a challenge. From the whodunits of the twenties and thirties to the whydunits and spy thrillers of more recent times, the puzzle is a principal ingredient. The best mysteries still offer readers a game as well as a story.

And what of the story? One thing can be guaranteed in mystery fiction, and is as true today as it was of the earliest Christie novels: it has the satisfying structure of a plot that is resolved. In the novel generally, there is no compunction on the writer to tell you everything that happened. How often do you hear complaints about novels that reach no conclusion whatsoever?

I think the other strong advantage of the Golden Age mysteries is that they have acquired a period charm. They are a window on a vanished age. It may be argued that they were never an accurate account of the way most people lived, but, accurate or not, those libraries and drawing rooms peopled with rich spinsters and majors and vicars and hosts of servants exist in the imagination. The values are rock solid: Right will always triumph over wrong, but what fun it will have been to have seen one of that society exposed as a blackguardly impostor!

So when I had got over my discovery that my fellow mystery writers were not ghouls, I began to understand how the best of them had adopted and adapted the real strengths of the old whodunit and created some of the most satisfying and exciting fiction being published in our time. Their concern is not with calibres of guns and temperatures of corpses; it is with the game they are playing with the reader, the need to construct a story that will work. And, most exciting, it is the opportunity the mystery gives them to describe a special world.

The possibilities are limitless. Dick Francis initiates the reader into the horse racing game; Robert van Gulik into ancient China; and Ed McBain into a tough police precinct in New York City. Within the strongly realized setting of the spy world, John le Carré explores the meaning of betrayal. James

McClure, with his Afrikaner detective and his Zulu colleague, conveys the social tensions in South African society without ever lecturing his readers. In *Stronghold,* Stanley Ellin shows a Quaker community invaded by one of its lost souls turned psychopath, and raises disturbing questions about the practicalities of faith. The mystery is not moribund; it is developing all the time. Have *you* thought of your own way of shaping its development? I hope I am persuading you to try.

My own interest is the mystery in a period setting, though I should say that I chanced on Victorian London almost accidentally. I was mainly interested in sport. It just happened that the sports event I used as background for *Wobble to Death* occurred in 1879. I am not an expert on the Victorian era, nor a history professor, just an inexhaustible collector of the trivia of times past. But, with *The False Inspector Dew,* I moved on to the nineteen-twenties, but I suppose I am still rooted in the past. Not so deeply, I hope, as this reader thought:

Dear Mr. Lovesey,
   I have read all of the Sergeant Cribb books with great enjoyment, but I did not write to tell you because I thought you were dead. My husband says he thinks you may still be alive. I suppose it does not really matter, but we would be most grateful to have this matter cleared up.

                                                    Yours sincerely,
                                                    s/Jennifer Y_____

Dear Mrs. Y_____,
   Thank you for your query as to whether I am a dead writer. I have sometimes wondered about this myself. But I cannot agree that it does not really matter. It matters to me and my wife, and my wife says she is sure I am still breathing. I hope this has cleared up the question.

                                                    Yours sincerely,
                                                    s/Peter Lovesey

14

MYSTERIES WITHIN MYSTERIES

by *Patricia Moyes*

AS A WRITER of mystery stories, the compliment I treasure most is when somebody says to me, "The characters in your books are so alive. They are just like real people." I find that this is often said on a note of faint surprise, as if the personages in a detective novel had no right to be anything more than cardboard puppets, dancing through the intricacies of the plot.

I have to admit that this surprise is sometimes justified. Some mystery authors seem content to sacrifice credibility of character to the speed and thrill of the action. Others—a more distinguished group—tend to create one splendidly rounded character in the person of their detective, who recurs in book after book, but they bother very little with the personalities of the supporting cast. For me, the reality of my people is tremendously important, and I like to think that my concern for them enhances the enjoyment of my readers.

"But," you may say, "a mystery novel should be fast-moving, baffling and exciting. Who wants to take time out for in-depth character studies and long descriptions of individual characters?"

Bringing characters to life

You are quite right. A long description will never bring a character to life in the mind of the reader. So, how is it to be done?

First, by what I can only call love and concern on the author's part. You have to take the time to think about your characters, until you know them like old friends. You should explore and discover far more about them than you will ever need to use in the book. Decide not only how they look, but how they dress, what they like to eat, what books they read, what their hobbies are. Above all, listen to them until you hear their voices in your mind.

This brings me to my second point. However well you may come to know your characters, it will do no good unless you have developed a technique for communicating your knowledge to your reader through the medium of the printed page. In my view, this is best achieved by dialogue.

Many excellent prose writers go all to pieces when they try their hands at dialogue. I think this comes about because writing dialogue takes a special discipline which they have never taken the time to study. There is a world of difference between words intended to be read, and words intended to be spoken, and, whether in a play or a book, all dialogue falls into the latter class. The writing of it is a technique, and it must be learned.

I wish I could simply recommend that every writer have the good luck I had—the chance to spend years working in the theater before I ever came to novel writing. Of course, that's not possible, but there is a lot you can do.

See as much professional theater as you possibly can. Don't just sit there and enjoy yourself; bring out your analytical faculties. Read the play both before and after you see it. Learn to distinguish among the various contributions which go to make up the production—those of the writer, the actor and the director. Remember that as a novelist your job will be even tougher than the dramatist's, for you will not have the benefit of a talented interpreter—a really good actor can make magic and touch his audience with the most banal of lines. Your dialogue will have to be good enough and punchy enough to make direct contact with your readers. If possible, join an amateur dramatic group and start looking at lines from the actor's viewpoint. You will very soon discover that there is a world of difference between dialogue that reads impressively, and dialogue that plays well. A critic once said about *The Taming of the Shrew,* "It's really a terrible play. The trouble is that it plays so superbly." Read your Shakespeare again, not as great literature, but as an actor's script. *He* knew all about dialogue.

Listen to people. Listen to everyone you meet, and take time to analyze your reactions. You will find that a great many of the opinions you form of people speaking are based not on what they say, but on how they say it.

For instance, that man in the railway train the other day. You classified him at once as fussy, self-centered, and a bit of an old woman. Why? He wanted the window closed. Well, there was nothing so strange about that; you were thinking of closing it yourself. All right, think back. He was reading a newspaper, and you noticed that instead of flapping the pages around like most people, he had folded it neatly into quarters in order to read his chosen piece. Then, he was already on his feet and closing the window before he spoke, and he certainly did not request your opinion. He said, "You don't mind if we have the window closed? I'm extremely prone to chills at this time of year."

One mannerism, one short sentence—and you had made up your mind as to the sort of man he was. You'll notice that it is not necessary to describe his appearance at all. Your readers will fill in the blanks for themselves.

How very different was that woman at the cocktail party.

"I'm Amanda Bickersteth. I've been *dying* to meet you. I've read *all* your books."

"I'm so—"

"Now, you must tell me exactly how you think up all those *marvelous* plots."

"Well, as a matter of—"

"That one set on the tropical island . . . you must know the Caribbean *inside out*. Come on now, do tell—which island was it really?"

"I don't—"

"Dwight and I go to St. Thomas every winter. Oh, I know *just* what you're going to say—it *is* crowded, but we just love it. Oh, dear, there's Dwight now. I'm afraid I must rush. It's been *so* interesting talking to you, I really feel I've learned *a lot* about writing . . . ."

You get the idea? One day, both those people will find a niche in one of your books.

"Creating" a work of fiction

This is not to say that you ever can or should take a real person and "put him into a book." Unless you are writing the story of his life, he will not fit conveniently into the mold of your plot. What's more, if you have a real-life model to draw from, you will always be asking yourself, "What would my friend do in these circumstances?" rather than, "What will my imaginary character do next?"

A work of fiction is a creation, and the people in it are, literally, your creatures. The man in the train and the woman at the party are no more than raw material, jottings in a notebook. (I don't keep one myself, except mentally, but many writers do and find it very useful.) One day, when you need a social chatterbox or an egocentric hypochondriac for your story or novel, a gesture or a phrase will emerge from your memory, digested and ready for use.

To return to the subject of dialogue. I advised you to listen until in your mind you could "hear" your people talking, and this is vitally important. Speak the lines of dialogue aloud— or else imagine them spoken by your character, in his or her voice and intonation. You will very soon find yourself thinking, "No, she wouldn't put it like that. She'd come straight to the point," or, "He wouldn't be able to resist being a bit long-winded over a thing like that." This may sound too easy, but I firmly believe that if every author followed those simple rules, a lot of books would be a great deal easier to read—and a lot of good novels could be transferred to the stage or the screen without the necessity for rewriting a lot of literally unspeakable dialogue.

"Defending" your plots

When I talk about getting to know your characters, I don't mean that you should hesitate to put pen to paper until you have mentally created at least half a dozen living, credible human beings. If you tried to do that, you would probably never start to write the book at all. It is here that we come close to the heart of what will always remain a mystery to me, and, I suspect, to many other writers. Does the writing create the character, or the character the writing? At what point is a fictional personality born? When does he or she become truly alive? All I can tell you is my own experience. My books start with a background—the place, the activity, the social ambience that forms the backdrop of the story. Secondly, I have to work out the plot like a problem in logic or mathematics.

At this stage, I freely admit, the characters are very shadowy indeed—a bloodless collection labeled "rich business-man," "social climber hostess," "ambitious young journalist," and so on. A stereotyped lot, to be sure, but most of us are stereotypes to strangers, who see us only from a distance. The closer we get to other people, the more their personalities begin to emerge from behind the convenient labels.

It is the same with fictional characters. As you write, listening all the time for those voices, remembering quirks of speech or behavior from real life, you will find your people stepping out of the shadows, revealing themselves in their own true personalities. If this sounds like a sort of miracle, I can only agree that it is just that. What is more, some of the stronger-minded characters are quite capable of taking your plot and twisting it to suit their own ideas. So far, I have managed to defend my basic plot structure—the murderer, the victim, the method, the motive, and the means of discovery—against all comers, but it has not always been easy. Designated murderers have developed such charm that they have nearly succeeded in talking themselves out of just retribution; victims can turn out to be so entertaining that I can hardly bear to part with their company early in the book.

With key characters like those, the author must either harden his heart or scrap the book and start again. Once you depart from your plot structure, you are lost, and your characters will fall with you. When it comes to the minor people in the story, however, it is a different matter. They grow from chapter to chapter like ivy up a wall. They become headstrong, stubborn, talkative, and possessive. They often behave in quite unexpected ways.

In my own novel writing I have had a young woman who simply refused to marry the eminently suitable young man I'd selected for her; a harsh, unsympathetic, middle-aged husband who turned out to be deeply and movingly in love with his young wife, although he could not find the way to tell her so; a serious-minded young bureaucrat who turned out to have a wickedly mischievous sense of humor that almost wrecked my plot (I should have been warned about him, because I had met his brother in an earlier book; frivolity obviously ran in the family).

As the author, of course, I could have simply forced all these characters to behave as I had originally intended them to do. This might have made my job somewhat easier—but it would have destroyed all my satisfaction in the work, because it would have withdrawn from my creatures the fragile breath of life which I had offered them, and which they had accepted. And, for sure, nobody would ever have paid me that nice compliment, "They are just like real people."

15

PLOTTING THE REALISTIC DETECTIVE NOVEL

by *Marcia Muller*

RECENTLY I WAS HAVING DINNER with a fellow writer, and for once we were not talking shop. Instead, we were discussing a mutual friend who was having problems. After a while my friend looked thoughtful and said, "Maybe we shouldn't be talking like this. After all, remember what Sharon said about her last case: You can't understand what goes on in another person's life unless you exist inside it."

Sharon is my private detective, Sharon McCone, who to date has appeared in ten novels. And what my writer friend didn't realize at the time was that she had just paid me one of the greatest compliments of my career. Her casual quoting of Sharon told me that I had created a real character and a real situation—ones that could be remembered and applied to situations in everyday life!

In the course of our reading we've all run across characters and stories that have such reality that we remember them long after we've forgotten our best friend from high school or what happened to us in the summer of '74. In many detective novels, we encounter situations so strange that any investigator would insist they couldn't possibly happen; yet we believe in them implicitly, cheer for the hero the whole way, and heave a sigh of relief when everything is finally resolved. What makes these stories so believable? Why do we remember some novels long after we turn the last page, while we dismiss others as mere gimmickry—and often don't bother to read to the end?

The answers to these questions lie in the novels' characters. A realistic detective novel is *not* about cardboard characters sitting around a drawing room, puzzling over mechanical clues to a bloodless murder. It *is* about real people who exist in a world that is not all that dissimilar to the reader's world. What happens to these people in the course of the novel is extraordinary, and their response to the events may be unusually courageous or clever, but the realistic backdrop against which they act convinces the reader that the story actually could happen.

Characters in context

To make your reader believe—and become involved in— the plot of your detective novel, not just your hero but also your villain and your secondary characters must be believable. These are the people who will develop as you plan and write your book; who will interact with one another; and whose actions will suggest plot twists, red herrings, or even a better ending than the one you had first envisioned.

The development of the plot of my seventh novel *There's Nothing To Be Afraid Of* is an example of how characters create a story. I wanted to write a book set in San Francisco's Vietnamese refugee community. I had researched the subject and knew that many of the refugees had been resettled in the Tenderloin district of the city—an area previously the sole turf of the poor and homeless, prostitutes and pimps, drug addicts and pushers. I knew that the refugees were changing the character of the neighborhood, and that the changes, while positive, had caused resentment and conflict with the long-time inhabitants. My research provided a factual basis from which I could begin to speculate: What if that resentment flared into violence—a campaign of terror directed against a group of Vietnamese living in one of the Tenderloin hotels? What if the campaign resulted in a murder? That, I decided, was the problem Sharon would be asked to investigate.

I now had a real setting for my novel and a situation that could very well occur in real life. I also had in mind several types of people who were likely to become involved in such a conflict, but I needed to create distinct characters. I made a list, named individuals, removed a few who didn't quite fit, added a few more. The final cast included a Vietnamese family, the Vangs; a street preacher, Brother Harry; a homeless man, Jimmy Milligan, who quoted poetry; a flower seller, Sallie Hyde; and a porno theatre owner, Otis Knox. But at this point, these were merely names on paper. Next, I had to make them real.

To be truly believable, every fictional character must have a past, a present, and hopes for the future. Some of these details may be relevant to your plot, some may not. Some you may reveal to your reader, others you may choose to conceal until the unraveling of your mystery. But you should be aware of all of them. They are what flesh out your characters, give them a frame of reference, and allow them to act and react to the situation around them. And in turn, the acting and reacting of the characters help you to structure your plot.

In writing the detective novel, it is essential to remember that you are not merely creating a sleuth, or a victim, or a criminal; instead, you are writing about a real flesh-and-blood person who also *happens* to be a sleuth, victim, or criminal. This person does not exist in a vacuum; he has a life outside of the immediate story, consisting of a family, home, romantic entanglements, friends, political opinions, food preferences, hobbies—and much more. You may choose not to bring in all of these facts—they may not be relevant—but you should be aware of them, since they may come in handy at some point in your book. For instance, Sharon is an amateur photographer, able to read negatives, a skill that allows her to discover the motive for the murder in her fourth case, *Games to Keep the Dark Away*. I did not invent this hobby merely for the purpose of solving that case; it was something I had always known about her, but I had not mentioned it in the earlier books because it was not relevant.

Creating an existing context for your character is particularly important in the case of a series character. When I began writing about Sharon McCone (several years and many abortive attempts before she finally saw print), I created a biography for her. This contained details about her family and upbringing, her educational and work history, and such other things as political leanings, likes and dislikes in food, what she finds attractive and unattractive in men, even color preferences and the style of furniture she favors. As the series has progressed, many of these details have altered, because in fiction, as in real life, people change in response to the conditions around them. For example, Sharon originally preferred modern furniture, but after a case involving Victorian houses, she recognizes a fondness for older things. And, as each of her cases brings her into contact with violent death and evil, she becomes more worldly-wise and perhaps a shade more cynical.

The milieu in which your character exists should also include details of home life and friends. Sharon once lived in a rundown studio apartment in San Francisco's Mission district; she bought a house in the Glen Park area and has the usual first-time homeowner's problems. At All Souls Legal Cooperative, she is surrounded by friends and co-workers: her boss, Hank Zahn; her close friend, tax attorney Anne-Marie Altman; Ted, the efficient secretary and intrepid worker of cross-word puzzles; Rae Kelleher, her assistant. In addition, she meets people through her cases: former lovers, Lt. Greg Marcus and Don DelBoccio; an antique dealer, Charlie Cornish—to name three who reappear from novel to novel. This supporting casts lends authenticity and often provides fodder for subplots or the main plot. These friends' actions and reactions affect Sharon, providing further impetus for character change, which is the stuff life—and a good story—are made of.

An example of character development from *There's Nothing To Be Afraid Of* may further clarify how this process works. Hoa Dinh never appears before the reader; he is a murder victim when we first see him. But it is essential that we know a great deal about him: first, because he has been murdered, and the motive for a murder is usually personal; and second, because the reader needs to care about Hoa in order to care about the search for his killer.

From my research about the Vietnamese refugees, I knew what Hoa's past and present typically would have been. On that factual basis, I built specific details. Hoa is only sixteen at the time of his death. He has fled Vietnam with his family, narrowly escaping drowning when their boat almost sank in the South China Sea; he has been shunted between refugee camps and temporary housing; he has finally achieved some stability in his permanent home in the Tenderloin, and is attending electronics classes. Hoa's hopes for the future are bright, but he is murdered before he can realize them. Hoa now has a past, present, and shattered future. He is now a tragic human being, not just an anonymous victim. Other details, concerning Hoa's feelings toward his present situation and the activities these feelings prompted, were essential to the unraveling of the plot and had to be concealed until the proper moment came to reveal them.

From unusual pasts to projected futures

I developed the other characters on my list in a similar manner, giving them unusual pasts, problematical presents, and in some cases, fears rather than hopes for the future. And eventually the circumstances of one of them suggested a motive for the harassment of the Vietnamese and the murder of Hoa Dinh. From that, I was able to project a tentative solution to the case.

The first five or six chapters of my novels are usually devoted to developing the situation and the characters and setting up complications. During this stage—even though I have the motive and solution firmly in mind—I like to keep the plot fairly flexible and open to change. The characters begin to act and interact, sometimes in unusual and surprising ways that suggest red herrings and further complications. These complications always lead to a richer plot than I've originally envisioned; often they can lead to a totally new solution. In *There's Nothing To Be Afraid Of,* the interaction between two characters in the subplot acted as a catalyst that enabled Sharon to put several pieces of information together, leading directly to the solution of the crime. I decided that the subplot would concern All Souls Legal Cooperative, Sharon's employer: A dissident group of attorneys is trying to wrest control of the co-op from the group that founded it.

My first character was Hank Zahn. I know Hank well: He is from an upper-middle-class background; he served in Vietnam, returned home disillusioned, and joined the protest movement. After law school, he founded All Souls. That is Hank's past. His present is troubled: Some of the attorneys want to "bring all Souls into the eighties" and do away with the concept of low-cost legal services for the underprivileged upon which the co-op was founded. Hank's hopes for the future are to continue serving his clients along those lines.

The other faction is led by Gilbert Thayer, a new partner. Gilbert's background is similarly privileged, but he is younger than Hank, has recently graduated from law school, and hopes to make a great deal of money. At present, he sees All Souls as a vehicle for furthering that ambition and is trying to turn it into a mainstream law firm—and do away with the sliding fee scale.

Given Gilbert's character, it is logical that he go about his plan in a bombastic, abusive manner—which he does. On the other hand, Hank has a low-key, contemplative personality. He withdraws to think things over and then emerges with a clever plan designed to force Gilbert's hand, resolving the situation at the co-op—and in doing so, providing Sharon with the nudge she needs to solve her case.

In the above example, both men act and react in ways that are logical and consistent with their particular frames of reference. Gilbert always blusters and alienates others; Hank always thinks things through and devises clever plans. It is this logic that makes the solution to the takeover attempt at All Souls believable.

Logical and realistic action

Your plot should always be based on your characters acting in ways that are logical with the past, present, and future you have devised for them. The body-finding scene (one of the most difficult to write in crime fiction) provides a good example of this. When Sharon McCone discovers a body, she does not panic, scream, or run away (as I might do), because she has discovered bodies before and is aware of what to do—check to see of the person is really dead. On the other hand, Sharon is an emotional woman, so she does not conduct herself casually or cooly at a murder scene; she feels and reacts with the appropriate seriousness and sadness.

How can you ensure that your characters are acting in a logical and realistic manner? The best way is to put yourself in their shoes, keeping in mind the frame of reference you have created for them. In *There's Nothing To Be Afraid Of,* one of the minor characters also finds a body. She is not a professional investigator, nor is she experienced with this sort of violent death, so she would not check the person's pulse and call the police as Sharon would. To figure out what her logical reaction would be, I first reviewed what I knew of the young woman: She was easily frightened, had a family to whom she was close, and was not overly trusting of the police. Then I put myself into the situation: It's dark, there's a dead person on the floor, I'm scared. What would *I* do—given this young woman's background? Panic and run to get help from my family, of course. And that's exactly what my character did.

In all your characters' actions—whether as momentous as those on finding a body or as simple as deciding what to have for breakfast—place yourself in the situation, *keeping in mind the person's particular frame of reference*. This is sure to help you come up with a logical reaction that will also move your plot along to a realistic conclusion.

In assessing how plausible the plot of your detective novel is, you may want to ask yourself the following questions: Is my story based—however loosely—upon actual fact? Have I created a situation that—given those facts—could probably happen? Are my characters representative of types who would be likely to become involved in such a situation? Have I developed them fully, with an eye to the larger context in which they live? Are their actions—and thus the movement of my plot—logical and consistent with their particular frames of reference?

Once you have answered "yes" to these questions, you will feel confident about allowing your characters' interactions to create the clues, red herrings, and plot twists that will make your plot truly baffling. These, however, are merely mechanics, and only as good as the people who discover the clues, fall for the red herrings, and untangle the twists. In the detective novel, the crime is only as interesting as the person who commits it and the person who solves it.

16 "HAD-I-BUT-KNOWN":
HOW TO USE IT IN
PLOTTING SUSPENSE NOVELS
by *Elizabeth Peters*

THAT DIABOLICALLY IRREVERENT versifier, Ogden Nash, is responsible for popularizing the phrase "Had I But Known" (HIBK for short) as a description of one school of detective fiction. Suspense fiction is supposed to be particularly prone to this weakness, and admittedly, its heroines often intone sentences beginning, "If I had but known what horrors lurked in the ancient hall of Castle Grimly . . ." But HIBK tricks are indispensable to all forms of suspense fiction.

The naïve narrator who hears a stealthy creak in the tower where the body lies, and nonchalantly proceeds to investigate it, is the subject of one of Nash's funniest verses. Humor aside, this is the most basic plot problem of the suspense novel. Without danger to the heroine, there is no suspense, and no story. If the heroine is a professional—police officer, spy, or private eye—the author need not explain why she decides to investigate. It is part of her job. But my heroines are mostly amateurs—people like you and me. This increases the strength of reader identification, but makes it difficult to construct a situation in which the girl is imperilled by forces she cannot control or escape. Let's invent a plot.

Our heroine, Jane Jones, is a young girl of good family,

beautiful, impoverished and upright, who accepts a position as governess in a remote part of England. After arriving at Castle Grimly, she experiences a series of terrifying events, culminating in an attempt on her life. Why doesn't she pack her portmanteau and leave?

Somewhat to my surprise (for my mind is not usually so orderly), the answers to this vital question fell neatly into outline form.

A. *She doesn't want to leave.*

1. She has fallen madly in love with the hero and cannot bear to leave him.

This is one of the most common motives used; it is also one of the weakest and least convincing. The *reader* is not madly in love with the hero, who is often moody, broody, scarred, and otherwise uncomfortable to be around. Modern readers lack patience with a girl so irrationally infatuated.

2. She loves, or feels a sense of responsibility for another character, often the child she has been hired to teach.

The only objection I have to this device is that it has been used so often. It can be used effectively, if the personalities of the heroine and the potential victim are properly developed. Mary Stewart did it splendidly in *Nine Coaches Waiting* by portraying a wistful, engaging child and a spunky, conscientious heroine. However, the danger to the child (aged grandmother, simple-minded youth) should arise legitimately from the exigencies of the plot, and not be attributable to a wandering homicidal maniac or kidnapper.

3. She has not accomplished the purpose for which she came to Castle Grimly.

In this case her purpose must be strong if she is willing to risk life and limb to achieve it. Clearing her unjustly imprisoned brother, discovering the fate of the sister who vanished at Grimly five years earlier, searching for her roots or her missing lover—such motives as these might impel a woman to investigate a funny noise in the tower, or do anything else necessary—but the motive must be established, or at least hinted at, before the action begins.

4. Her own survival or sanity depends on solving the mystery of Castle Grimly.

This is another commonly used trick, and its effectiveness varies (and what does not?) with the skill of the writer. I tried to use this, combined with point #2 above, in a contemporary ghost story, *Ammie Come Home*. The person threatened was the niece of my middle-aged heroine, whom she loved like a daughter; and since the threat was supernatural, its early manifestations were vague enough to be written off as bad dreams or hallucinations. By the time the heroine realized that her niece was possessed by the spirit of a former occupant of Castle Grimly (a house in Georgetown, in this case), the damage had been done; the threat would follow wherever they went, and the only hope of escape was to find the cause of the haunting.

5. She doesn't realize until too late that she is threatened.

There are difficulties in the method. If the threat is so vague that the heroine doesn't sense it, the reader may not notice it either. Conversely, if by clues and plants, the reader is made aware of approaching peril as he ought to be, the heroine would be pretty stupid to miss those hints. I find dreams and similar portents extremely useful in this context; they can be intensely horrifying, but not actively threatening.

6. For reasons of egotism and/or consummate curiosity, the heroine appoints herself amateur detective.

This is probably the weakest excuse of all, though I have used it many times myself. One of my favorite heroines, Amelia Peabody, in *Deeds of the Disturber, Mummy Case, Lion in the Valley, Crocodile on the Sandbank*, and *The Curse of the Pharaohs*, is a pushy, opinionated woman who consistently rushes into danger, because she is convinced she can do the job—any job—better than anyone else.

There are other reasons why the heroine might not want to leave Castle Grimly, but I think that gives you the idea. Let's proceed to point B.

B. *The heroine cannot leave.*
1. She is physically isolated. She may be on an island and the villain has destroyed all the boats. Or perhaps a flood has devastated the countryside, so that roads, telephones, etc., are unusable. One of my heroines found herself in a distant part of the Scottish Highlands, with a blizzard raging, just when she had (belatedly, I admit) made up her mind to leave. Clearly, it is easier to arrange such isolation if you set your novel in an earlier century, when methods of transportation and communication were more primitive. But even in a modern setting it can be done, if you invent an earthquake or volcanic eruption, or if you have placed your heroine in a remote village in Greece, for example.

2. She is isolated by social or political circumstances.

Few places in this day and age are so physically remote that there is no telephone or village constable available. But if the heroine is unfamiliar with the language—if she has no local sponsors who can vouch for her sanity and her honesty—if she is in some part of the world where women are second-class citizens—under such circumstances it is possible to construct a plot in which she must rely on her own wits and strength.

3. She is isolated by legal barriers.

The most conspicuous examples of such restrictions are the legal inequities affecting women in England and America during the early Victorian period. During most of the nineteenth century, women could not vote, hold office, or attend professional schools or universities. More to the point for the writer of romantic suspense fiction is the fact that they could not own property or get a divorce, even in cases of physical abuse.

The classic example of such mistreatment can be seen in *The Woman in White* (1860)—my favorite romantic suspense novel—by Wilkie Collins. His heroine was vulnerable because English law gave her husband absolute control over her property and her person.

4. She is imprisoned—locked in her room or in the dungeons of Castle Grimly.

This probably won't work for an entire book. In *The Count of Monte Cristo,* Dumas described at great length his hero's attempts to break out of prison; but no matter how ingenious you are, it is unlikely that you can sustain interest in this device for three hundred pages. However, I would love to see someone pull it off.

5. She is too shy, intimidated, or neurotic to fight back to try to escape.

Personality disorders of this sort are common, even in this liberated age. I fear, however, that in this case truth is too unconvincing for fiction. Readers are not inclined to sympathize with such an insipid female. The primary weakness in Daphne DuMaurier's modern classic *Rebecca* is that the shy, unworldly heroine arouses more irritation than pity.

One step removed from this problem, but related to it, is the plot development of another form of suspense story, in which the heroine, instead of investigating the tower where the body lies, or its equivalent, takes to her heels and flees the villain. It is the feminine version of the "chase" story, and here, as in the first type, the difficulty is one of motivation: Why does she run from danger into danger instead of stopping at the nearest police station?

I. *She loses her wits and runs off in panic.*

Forget this one. It may be what you or I would do, but it is not acceptable behavior for a heroine. Not only is it lazy technique, but it smacks of male chauvinism—"you know how women are; they lose their heads in a crisis." Modern women readers won't buy this, nor should they.

Mind you, a number of famous male heroes have succumbed to this very weakness. In John Buchan's masterpiece, *The Thirty-Nine Steps,* the hero, Richard Hannay takes off in mindless flight after finding a body in his sitting room. Hannay is a strong macho male and a member of the sacred upper class; his explanation of why the murdered man happened to be in his flat might have raised a few eyebrows at Scotland Yard, but could not possibly have resulted in his arrest. Any reader who has followed his marvelous adventures has no cause for complaint, but a heroine who behaved in such a rattlebrained fashion would undoubtedly be blasted by the critics. Buchan gets away with it because of the grace and style of his writing (and perhaps because critics are more tolerant of irrational behavior in a hero than in a heroine?), but unless you are able to replicate Buchan's strengths, you should not copy his weaknesses.

II. *Her credibility is in doubt; the police will not believe her.*

a. She herself is a suspect in a murder or bank heist, or whatever crime you chose to invent.

The circumstantial evidence against her must be strong, or she will be guilty of point I (above)—mindless flight. It's not hard to set up such a plot. Perhaps the real murderer has framed her, planting the bloodstained knife in her lingerie drawer, or luring her to the scene of the crime by means of a spurious message. Alternatively, she may be fortuitously involved because of a strong motive (and no alibi) or because of a history of mental instability, a previous criminal record, or the like.

b. The reason she is being pursued is not known even to her; she can't possibly hope to convince the police.

Again, there are two sub-variants. The first may arise

from a pre-existing fact of which the heroine is not aware; for example, she is the true heir to millionaire Uncle Donald's estate. Or else her danger stems from what I call the "initiating coincidence" that sets a suspense plot moving. My heroines are always running into people who thrust mysterious parcels or cryptic messages into their unwilling hands. My novel *Legend in Green Velvet* began with a case of mistaken identity. The conspirator, a rather confused elderly gentleman, passed his message to the wrong woman. I tried to use a variant of the chase technique by having the heroine pursue the conspirator, to try to give him back his parcel. In the meantime, she is herself pursued by assorted villains who also want the parcel. Though my heroine quite properly calls the police when her room is ransacked, it does not occur to her or to them that the innocent-looking parcel can be responsible for the break-in.

c. The events that convince her she is in danger are so preposterous no one would credit them.

I like this trick because I like to invent preposterous circumstances. When my middle-aged heroine in *Copenhagen Connection* disappears, presumably kidnapped, her friends cannot convince the police she needs help, because the ransom note does not demand money; it asks for "Margaret's bathrobe."

d. The pursuer has the law on his side. Mary Stewart used this in *Madam, Will You Talk?* The presumed villain was the father of the child Stewart's heroine wanted to protect. She had excellent reasons for believing him to be a threat to the child, but she had no legal right to interfere.

e. The villains are in such hot pursuit that the girl doesn't have time to stop and explain the situation.

This works best when combined with several of the other points mentioned. The more unbelievable the circumstances, the longer it will take the heroine to make a convincing case. The farther she is from home, the less likely it is that her story will be believed.

f. She has reason to suspect that the police official or the entire police force is involved in the crime.

Unhappily, this is a convincing argument these days, when the average newspaper reader is only too well acquainted with tales of police corruption or brutality. Again, it works well when combined with other factors, such as that of isolation: A woman in a foreign country whose legal code is strange to her may be reluctant to trust the local sheriff. Or perhaps she has observed the sheriff in friendly conversation with her pursuer. . . .

The girl *must* go to the tower where the body lies. She *must* be in danger. What counts is *why* she goes.

Overlooked clues

Now, I would like to discuss another basic Had-I-But-Known device—the clue that is overlooked or misinterpreted by a heroine who laments, "Had I but known. . . ."

It might seem that clues are not essential to a suspense novel, at least not to the same degree as in the straight detective story. In some types of suspense fiction, such as the chase tale, clues may be dispensed with. The reader doesn't care who the villains are or why they are in pursuit; he is interested only in the protagonist's efforts to escape. But in many suspense stories, there is a mystery to be solved or a plot to be uncovered before the heroine can relax—in the arms of the hero or elsewhere, as she prefers. Bright readers like to exercise their wits as well as their emotions. They know, when they read my books, that there will usually be a happy ending. But if they can anticipate the method by which that ending is to be achieved they will be more pleased with themselves and with me. They have a right to expect clues that will enable them to work out at least part of the answer; and if the story is not to come to a premature end, those clues must be suppressed or ignored by the heroine. The writer's challenge is to invent valid reasons for the girl's failure to employ those clues to protect herself. Here are a few examples of some of the clues employed in successful romantic suspense fiction and how to deal with them.

A. *The classic clue,* used in all forms of mystery fiction.

1. Facts or objects deliberately suppressed by the heroine, thus obfuscating the solution: the bloodstained handkerchief, the murder weapon, the initialed cigarette case under the body.

Do try to avoid these. They have been overused to the point of caricature, and they never were very convincing. If the heroine really suspects that her lover has slaughtered kindly old Grandma Smith, she has no business trying to protect him, and if she is sure he is innocent, she ought to realize that she may be making matters worse: The concealed object may contain a clue to the real murderer. If you must use this hoary old device, at least make sure the girl destroys the evidence completely: Be certain the bloodstained handkerchief is totally consumed in the library fireplace, or that the gun won't turn up again under even more damning circumstances. She should also check to see that the library door is closed and that none of the servants is peeking through the keyhole.

2. Clues overlooked or misinterpreted. The difficulty is that the clue must be hidden so neatly that even an intelligent heroine will logically overlook it. A number of the methods used in the straight detective story to accomplish this can be used successfully in suspense novels, too.

The easiest method is to admit the reader into the confidence of someone other than the protagonist—perhaps the villain himself. In *The Chocolate Cobweb,* by Charlotte Armstrong, the reader actually watches the murderer manipulating the mechanism by which the heroine is to be annihilated. No one else in the house knows about the device, so hero and heroine cannot be blamed for failing to anticipate its use, and the suspense of the reader is heightened as he watches the girl unwittingly walk toward her doom.

Comment by an omniscient narrator (the author) is another way of planting a clue that is known to the reader but is justifiably ignored by the heroine. I did this in *Black Rainbow,* where it seemed particularly appropriate since the book is a Victorian thriller; the technique is typical of the writing of that period. "It was not Jane's fault that she missed the real significance of the incident. She was now too far removed from the world in which such ideas still lingered, passed on from father to son and mother to daughter, fading slowly with the passage of the centuries but ready to leap up like a smoldering fire when fresh kindling is added." The purplish prose and the hints of uncanny peril are in keeping with Victorian melodrama, and are typical HIBK technique.

The most difficult and most craftsmanlike method of planting an obscure clue is to tell a straight story, without interpolations from minor characters or the author, and to bury the evidence. For example:

a) The casual comment. The pertinent statement, seemingly irrelevant, but actually vital to the solution, is buried by hiding it in a mass of verbiage. I find this easy to do since my characters are hopelessly loquacious. In *Street of the Five Moons,* my heroine missed an essential clue—an admission, by the hero, that he had entertained various ladies in his hotel room—because she was jealous; they were arguing; and the villains were pounding at the door. Anyone might be excused for being distracted under such circumstances. Later, when things had calmed down, she remembered the remark, and was able to deduce the identity of the Master Criminal.

b) The esoteric clue—information so obscure that only a specialist in the subject can interpret its significance. This is contemptible. I have often made use of it. But don't underestimate your readers; a few of them will spot the clue and will pat themselves on the back for their cleverness. Readers of my supernatural romances have learned to be suspicious of any group of nine people: It may turn out to be a witches' coven.

You can give the impression that you are playing fair if you interpret the esoteric clue as you plant it. In *Curse of the Pharaohs*, I use an ancient fairy tale to point directly to the identity of the killer; although I analyzed the story in painstaking detail, its specific applications eluded most readers.

B. *Clues, dire hints and portents particularly applicable to the romantic suspense novel.*

1. Concealing the identity of the hero.

This is important, not only to the romance, but to the suspense. The actions of male characters may be deliberately ambiguous, and if the heroine trusts the wrong man, she may be asking for a sojourn in the dungeons of Castle Grimly. I am beginning to suspect I do not hide clues of this nature as well as I ought; my hero is only too often the man the heroine particularly dislikes at the beginning of the book. Such insight need not destroy the reader's enjoyment of the story, but it is essential that the writer account logically for behavior that may lead the heroine into a mistaken identification.

In my novel *Witch*, I had two separate cases of mistaken identity. The real hero of the book departed in chapter one and did not re-enter the story until the moment of crisis, several hundred pages later. It was necessary to remind the reader of his existence, so I had the heroine stare dreamily at his picture, write and receive letters from him, and so on. The other candidate for the position of hero was on the spot, being charming to the heroine. Not only was he the villain, he was one of the nastiest I have ever invented, and one of his victims had to appear villainous until virtually the end of the book. The real villain committed several of the criminal acts attributed to the victim, whose reputation he had carefully destroyed. Other situations were set up by the villain in such a way that the victim's acts were misinterpreted by witnesses. One of the points I wanted to make was the degree to which preconceptions and prejudices influence the interpretation of a given act.

2. The classic, flat-out "Had-I-But-Known" label, which identifies the statement in question as vital to the solution. In effect, the writer is saying, "Here's the clue—what do you think I'm going to do with it?"

This differs from the clue that is planted by the omniscient narrator in that it is voiced by the protagonist, who speaks in the first person. There are two things to avoid like the plague in using this device. First, don't use the phrase "had I but known," unless you do it satirically. Second, avoid the obvious, "had I but known the smoking pistol was the murder weapon, I would never had hidden it in my knitting bag." Only an idiot could miss the implications of a smoking pistol at the scene of a murder.

At one point in *Borrower of the Night,* when my detective heroine finds a peculiar little golden image, "a dark and elusive memory stirred unpleasantly in the back of my mind—stirred and subsided, like a slimy thing in a swamp." The words "had I but known" are not used, but they are implicit—and the reader knows this object is going to be an essential clue. The old master, Wilkie Collins, was particularly good at this sort of thing. Here is the comment of the family lawyer, after he has drawn up the heroine's marriage settlement, in *The Woman in White:*

"No daughter of mine should have been married to any man alive under such a settlement as I was compelled to make for Laura Fairlie." This is HIBK at its best and most effective.

"Had I but known" is a lament we all utter, only too often, in the course of normal life. Had I but known the cat was going to jump onto the mantel I wouldn't have left my favorite Sèvres vase up there. Had I but known the man standing on the corner was an escaped thief, I wouldn't have neglected to lock the car. . . . If the writer can play on this human weakness, he gains strongly in reader sympathy and reader identification. However, people tend to forget their mistakes; they don't want to identify with average idiots like themselves (or me). It is perilously easy for a writer to go too far in depending on human weakness to excuse his protagonist's mistakes. The feeling he wants to evoke in the reader is not "I wouldn't be stupid enough to do a thing like that," but rather, "I do that sort of thing myself when I get rattled." So don't avoid the HIBK tricks. Use them correctly, and you will acquire a whole boxful of tools that can increase the effectiveness of your supsense novel.

17

"BUT THAT'S IMPOSSIBLE!"
by *Bill Pronzini*

SUPPOSE A MAN walks into the sixteenth-floor suite of an attorney one morning, is admitted to the lawyer's private office, and ten minutes later two witnesses hear a gunshot from within. Suppose these witnesses have the presence of mind to lock the only door immediately after the crime, thereby trapping the visitor in that one room. Suppose the police, when they arrive, find the attorney dead of a gunshot wound and the visitor alone with the body. And suppose a subsequent search of the man, of the office, and of the grounds sixteen stories below proves conclusively that no weapon exists anywhere.

You might say, "But that's impossible!"

What if a detective is hired to guard some two hundred expensive presents at a swanky wedding reception? What if the presents have been placed in a room whose windows are all locked and which has been searched by the detective and found to be uninhabited? What if later he is sitting in the hallway, watching the locked (and only) door to the room, when suddenly he hears the sound of glass shattering—and upon breaking down the door he finds one gift box open on the floor, empty of the valuable ring it had contained? And what if he also finds the largest of the windows broken and all the glass shards on the outside lawn, indicating that the window had been smashed *from the inside?*

Again you might say, "But that's impossible!"

In both cases, however, you would be wrong. For in the world of the "impossible crime" story, nothing is impossible. Guns *can* cease to exist inside locked offices after a murder; windows *can* be mysteriously broken under the nose of the keenest detective.

Solving crime puzzles

It has been said that Americans love puzzles. The crime puzzle, of which the impossible is the purest form, concerns itself not only with whodunit, but with howdunit. It is a conundrum for the connoisseur. Solving crime puzzles provides a good deal of satisfaction for the reader and offers the reassurance of order in a sometimes chaotic world. The more difficult the enigma, the greater the satisfaction in solving it. But the ultimate gratification belongs not to the solvers of the puzzles, but to the writer who, like a magician, can outwit even the most experienced and clever puzzle addict through misdirection, manipulation, and skillful sleight-of-hand.

Does such a prospect appeal to you? If so—if you like puzzles, enjoy reading and writing mystery stories, and have an inventive imagination—you possess the basic tools to write an impossible crime story. With these tools, and with a working knowledge of the form and the observance of a few important rules, you can create your own salable mystery. And your own high-point of satisfaction.

The most important technical requirement, as with any genre or sub-genre, is a thorough understanding of what the impossible is and what it should and should not be. Before you attempt to write one of your own, you should read those created by the form's best writers past and present, and become conversant with its history, its classics, and its clichés. The basic impossible story theme is the murder of someone, or the disappearance of someone or something, from a locked room or other closed (or, conversely, wide-open) space. There have been a vast number of variations on this theme, and variations on the variations, since the first locked-room novel, Israel Zangwill's *The Big Bow Mystery*, was published in 1892. (The first locked-room short story, Poe's "The Murders in the Rue Morgue," appeared a half-century before that.) What may strike the uninformed writer as a brilliant gimmick or variant may in fact have been used in a book or books fifty years ago—and would bring an instant rejection from knowledgeable editors if reused today.

The Grand Master of the impossible was John Dickson Carr, who wrote dozens of novels and short stories during his 40-year career, nearly all of which make use of one or more ingenious impossibles. His novel, *The Three Coffins*, is notable not only for a pair of masterful crime puzzles, but for its "locked-room lecture"—with an entire chapter (#17) devoted to a study of the ways and means in which a murder may take place, or appear to take place in a locked room.

Each of these basic methods is discussed at length in the chapter, but to whet your interest I'll list them in brief here:

1. The crime is not murder, but a series of coincidences ending in an accident that looks like murder.

2. It is murder, but the victim is impelled to kill himself or to die an accidental death.

3. It is murder, by a mechanical device already planted in the room and hidden undetectably in some innocent-looking piece of furniture.

4. It is suicide, which is intended to look like murder.

5. It is a murder which derives its problem from illusion and impersonation.

6. It is a murder which, although committed by somebody outside the room at the time, nevertheless seems to have been committed by somebody who must have been inside.

7. It is a murder depending on an effect exactly the reverse of number 5; that is, the victim is presumed to be dead long before he actually is.

Also discussed in the chapter are ways of gimmicking

doors and windows so that they seem to have been locked from the inside. Delivered by Carr's rotund and brilliant detective, Dr. Gideon Fell, the "locked-room lecture" is invaluable to anyone who intends to write an impossible crime story.

A vital nonfiction book is Robert Adey's *Locked Room Murders*—an exhaustive bibliography, complete with plot summaries and historical commentary, of more than 1300 "impossible" novels and short stories appearing throughout the world in the past eighty years. It was published in England by a small press (Ferret Fantasy) in 1979. An updated version is scheduled for publication late in 1990. (It should be noted that this book not only summarizes plots, but also provides, in a separate section, summaries of the solutions as well. This section should not be consulted until you have read the works in question, particularly those of John Dickson Carr, Clayton Rawson, and other experts. Peeking at the answers to puzzles is neither fair nor satisfying, after all, nor is it instructive.)

Rules and tools

Once you have become well-versed in the background of the impossible story, and you're ready to begin plotting one of your own, you should keep in mind the following general rules. You *can* sell an impossible if you break one of these rules (I've done so myself), but your chances will be considerably lessened. And you *can't* sell any story that breaks two or more.

Originality. As noted earlier, the number of variations already used is large; to repeat any of them, without offering a unique variation-on-a-variation, is to meet with immediate rejection. Your thorough study of the form will help to eliminate this problem. So will imagination. Remember, *nothing* is impossible in the realm of the impossible. Although the number of used variations is large, the number of unused variations is infinite; you can make your murder, theft, or disappearance as different or amazing or spectacular as you like. The more unusual and baffling it is, the more easily you'll find a home for it in print.

Plausibility. This is an adjunct of originality and just as important. No matter how far-fetched, how unusual, your plot may seem to be *on the surface,* it must have a wholly logical explanation. The gimmick can be improbable—a number of John Dickson Carr's wonderful plots are improbable—but like every one of Carr's plots and devices, it must nonetheless be plausible. The reader must be able to maintain his suspension of disbelief, to say to himself at the denouement, "Yes, that *could* happen."

Do not use such devices as secret panels, trap doors, door bolts turned from outside by means of pliers or string, daggers made of ice, exotic poisons, acrobatic midgets, or trained monkeys. Gimmicks like this were the staple of some detective-story writers in the early 1900s but by today's standards they are both hackneyed and implausible. If you can't think of a more original explanation for a locked-room murder than a secret panel through which the murderer entered and escaped, you'd better try your hand at a different type of story.

Simplicity. The plot of your story may be as intricate as you care to make it, but the impossible itself—the gimmick, the method behind the mysterious occurrence—should be kept simple. Any contrivance requiring more than a couple of pages or a large amount of technical jargon to explain should be avoided. Most real-life murders are relatively simple affairs; most classic locked-room fictional murders (or disappearances) are relatively simple, too. It is the artistry of the writer, the manipulation of events to create the illusion of complexity, that permits the crime to take on its fantastic qualities.

For this reason, you should shy away from the use of complicated mechanical devices. These strain credibility and require too much explanation. Also avoid the criminal mastermind who invents an ornate and involved contrivance when it would have been much easier for him to commit his crime in a straightforward fashion. It is much more believable to make the culprit an average, if clever, individual with simple criminal motives: to provide himself with an alibi, to conceal something, to take advantage of a given situation, to make it look as though someone else is guilty. It is not necessary, in fact, for the villain to plan an impossible crime; an elementary murder plot can turn into an "impossible" (as Carr demonstrates in his *Three Coffins* lecture), by coincidence or accident.

Fair play. The preponderance of impossibles are detective stories; the puzzles are solved by a detective who follows clues, uses his powers of observation, and arrives at the truth by logical deduction. If your story falls into this category, you must remember to give the reader the same opportunity to solve the enigma that you give your detective. He must be privy to the same clues as the investigator, and you must not withhold any important facts or supply him with deliberate misinformation. Readers don't mind being fooled, but they want to be fooled fair and square.

The illusion of incredibility

To illustrate these four rules, as well as the structure of the impossible crime story, I offer the solutions to the two crime puzzles I postulated at the beginning of this article. The premises are those of a pair of my own stories first published, some years apart, in *Ellery Queen's Mystery Magazine*. The first, "Proof of Guilt" (the disappearing gun), came into being as the result of a question I asked myself one morning: "How could someone shoot someone else in a locked room and then get rid of the weapon without himself leaving the room?" The first thing that occurred to me was, "What if he *ate* it?" A facetious and preposterous notion, of course . . . or is it?

Suppose the victim was shot not with an ordinary gun but with a homemade weapon, a sort of zip gun made of several component parts which could, after using, be broken down again into those separate components. Suppose the murderer was a drifter who had worked at a number of odd jobs, but there is a four-year gap in his past that he refuses to discuss. And suppose the police discover an old poster that explains his whereabouts during those four years—an old carnival sideshow poster bearing the words: STEAK AND POTATOES AND APPLE PIE ARE OUR DISH; NUTS, BOLTS, PIECES OF WOOD, BITS OF METAL IS HIS! THE AMAZING MR. GEORGE, THE MAN WITH THE CAST IRON STOMACH.

Now the idea of a gun-eating villain is no longer either facetious or preposterous; improbable, perhaps, but plausible nonetheless. The sideshow poster quoted above is not unveiled until the third-to-last paragraph of the story, and the final line reveals that the murderer had, indeed, eaten the zip gun after the shooting. (This particular impossible is an example of one in which the fair-play rule does not apply. The detective-narrator does not solve the crime until it is too late to do anything about it, and then only by turning up the poster. The emphasis is on the surprise revelation of the gun having been ingested, not on deduction.)

"A Nice Easy Job" was born while I was reading a mystery novel in which a policeman solved a murder by looking at a broken window and observing that there were no glass shards on the floor inside the room, when the culprit claimed that it had been broken from outside. "Whenever you break a window," the detective said, "the glass will always fall in the opposite direction. All these shards are outside; therefore this window was broken from within."

This fact happens to be true—under normal circumstances. But, I asked myself, was there a way to break a window from the outside so that all the shards would fall *toward* the person? And I discovered that there was. A strong man could attach a suction clamp—one of those bar-type gadgets with rubber cups at each end, like the ones used in the film *Topkapi* to lift a heavy glass case—and then lock it down so that the cups are securely suctioned to the glass. By giving the clamp a hard, rocking jerk or two, he could then break the window and have all the shards fall in his direction.

With my basic impossible worked out, I devised the set of circumstances in which a valuable ring would be stolen from a locked room the Nameless Detective was guarding. The thief perpetrated the crime in such a fashion to make it seem that "Nameless" had broken down the door in order to steal the ring itself; by the detective's own testimony, the room containing the wedding presents was empty and nobody, it is subsequently established, could have gotten in or out of the room through the broken window.

By deduction and clue-gathering (this one *is* a formal detective story), "Nameless" discovers that the ring had been stolen sometime earlier, when he and the culprit and three other men were in the room. What the thief had done was to palm the ring from a small ring box as he was replacing it in the larger gift box. Later, after breaking the window with the suction clamp, he threw a small bogus present in through the opening from outside, knocked the gift box off the table, and thereby created the illusion that it had been dislodged when the ring was stolen.

Like most successful impossibles, these two of mine seem obvious when finally explained. It is the structuring of them, remember, the sleight-of-hand, that turns them into puzzles and gives them the appearance of incredibility. And makes them so satisfying, too.

The impossibilities are limitless. . . .

18

THE SHORT WAY TO CRIME
by *Ian Stuart*

WRITING SHORT CRIME FICTION is much like writing any other sort of short story, but it does make some special demands of its own.

Writing any short story calls for different techniques from those used in writing novels or plays. Obviously. For one thing, the author has about a twentieth as many words at his disposal.

Also, there are rules that we break at our peril.

Over the years I have picked up some of these guidelines, and generally I try to observe them: 1) plots should be simple, 2) settings few, 3) the time span short, 4) descriptions brief, and, most important of all, 5) the characters few and strongly drawn.

Two and a half decades ago, I spent some time writing serials and short stories for newspapers and women's "pulp" magazines. It was human interest stuff, some of it with a "crime" element, and up to a point it was excellent training. I say up to a point, because if one does too much of that type of story, one can come to devise plots to a formula and to write in a way that is almost a sort of shorthand. One day when I first started writing, I was talking with an editor who suddenly broke in with, "What sort of shoe polish does X use?" I hadn't a clue. The question had never occurred to me, and, if it had, it wouldn't have seemed to be of overwhelming interest to me, let alone to anybody reading the story.

"You have to know your characters right through," he told me. "Everything about them." Where they went to school, what sports they play, what food they like may not come into the tale, but building up a detailed picture of your characters in your own mind helps you make them real to your readers. Besides which, it enables you to introduce touches that give the depth and color that bring a story alive. A seemingly casual reference to something in the past may explain a trait of character.

Having strong characters doesn't mean that you have to bang them onto the page like Mike Tyson flattening an opponent, nor does it mean that they have to be Mike Hammer look-alikes. What it does mean is that their basic characters are quickly recognizable, and the reader will feel empathy with them, or immediate dislike. The challenge is to use firm brush strokes, while hinting at subtleties there isn't space to describe.

Can you have a "bad" hero?

It is probably true that it takes experience and technical know-how to get away with a really "bad" hero in a novel, especially a crime novel. Mystery fiction has been called the twentieth-century equivalent of the medieval morality plays, and we are told repeatedly that one of the things readers like about it is that right always triumphs in the end, and the villain gets his comeuppance. Well, nearly always. To have a central character who is basically bad is to fly in the face of all that accumulated wisdom. Patricia Highsmith has done it with Tom Ripley *(The Talented Mr. Ripley),* and so have other authors with their characters, but for most novelists, it is probably safer to have heroes who, while possessing their share of human failings, are at least fundamentally on the side of the angels. Perversely, of course, it is their failings that account for a lot of their appeal; perfection in characters is not only boring, but it arouses an instinctive antagonism in those of us who haven't achieved such heights.

There is another point in favor of a basically decent leading character: the inescapable fact that a large percentage of heroes are their authors' fantasy projections of themselves, and I'm not talking only about first novels. If we are to follow the admonition to "write about what we know," we know more about ourselves than anyone else. Heroes are often their writers' wish fulfillment. After all, it is only human nature to want to see oneself in a favorable light.

At the same time, it is probably easier for a writer to get away with an unpleasant hero or heroine in a short story, perhaps because the reader doesn't have as long as he has in a novel to dwell on the character, to identify with him or her. And it's amusing for the author—that timid, law-abiding paragon of all virtue—to see things for a little while from the viewpoint of the wrong-doer. A case of sublimation, perhaps. Similarly, a detached and cynical attitude on the part of the writer may be amusing and acceptable in a short story, whereas it would be tedious spread over 70,000 words in a novel.

The vital first paragraph

Being boring in print is an author's worst sin. The reader will forgive him almost anything but the knowledge that reading the story was not only tedious, but a waste of time— which is one reason a short story has to make its impact quickly, and mystery short stories more so than most. The opening paragraph of any work of fiction is important; in the crime short story, it is doubly so, and it is worthwhile for a writer to spend a good deal of time and thought to get the opening right.

In your early days as a fiction writer, it is a good idea to plan your story before you start writing it, but some of us find that hard to do. When I start a story, I have only a rough idea of the outline. By the time I finish, the plot has usually changed at least once.

As a general rule, it's advisable to avoid long sentences, but remember that a succession of short sentences of virtually the same length makes very tedious reading. Short sentences build up the tension for a climax, while longer ones create a more tranquil mood. As in any writing, rhythm is extremely important. Try reading what you have written aloud—to yourself! That is a much better way of finding out whether the story reads well than scanning it quickly. Dialogue mustn't waffle. It needn't be quick-fire (a critic once complained that Noel Coward's characters talked like typewriters), but it must be concise. It may even be witty.

Keep description to a minimum. If you're writing a lyrical piece about a young girl's first sight of Venice, fine; you can let yourself go. But if you're writing an action story, most description is superfluous. It holds up the plot, and the reader may feel cheated or bored. There was a time when mystery shorts could run to 15,000 words, or even more, but nowadays few exceed 5,000 words, and if you use up a lot of space on description, it doesn't leave a great deal for action.

Actually, that's one of the rules I like to bend a little: I don't write "hard-boiled" tales, and judiciously used description can heighten tension as well as build up the background. In a story called "The Approach of Winter," which I wrote for *Ellery Queen's Mystery Magazine* a few years ago, the first 600 words or so are virtually all description. I wanted to set the scene and the atmosphere in a tiny village in the French Pyrenees in the off-season, because it was important to the action that followed. And, of course, properly handled, description can be used to lull the reader into a false sense of security before a big dramatic shock.

Use description to create atmosphere, but don't waste it. Don't indulge in details of a room or a character's clothes unless they are important to the plot. It may be sufficient to describe a person in only one or two words, such as "attractive" or "mean looking," leaving the reader to visualize him or her in his mind's eye. But be sparing with adjectives, "the enemies of nouns," which used too freely not only spoil the rhythm and weaken the impact, but can impede the action.

Plots without distractions

As I have said, a plot should be simple. In a short story, it should proceed without distractions; side issues only diffuse the reader's interest. There may be a twist in the ending, but it mustn't seem contrived; it must come naturally out of what has gone before. A plot in which the hero is arrested for a crime he didn't commit and cannot defend himself because it would mean revealing the one he did is now regarded as too hackneyed to be acceptable.

The micro short—the story of less than a thousand words that depends almost entirely on a twist at the end for its effect—has virtually disappeared, and now almost all short stories run between 1,500 and 6,000 words. The shortest ones have to be pared to the bone. One magazine editor recently laid down these guidelines: "stories of 1,500 words; whodunits or howdunits; no gratuitous violence, explicit sex, graphic language, seamy settings, grotesque crimes, or foreign settings."

Don't worry about length when you set out to write. There is a saying that every story has its own length, and the secret is in finding it. That sometimes comes with experience. Write out your tale, then revise it—again and again, if necessary—deleting everything that doesn't contribute to the effect you are trying to achieve. It's been said that if a writer is particularly impressed with a passage he's written, he should cut it out: The odds are that it's bad. Hard advice to take, perhaps, and few of us follow it!

Using description before introducing a dramatic shock is really a way of giving your story contrast. Evil is far more effective when it surfaces in a peaceful village setting than in a city slum, and unmasking a timid mouse of a sister as the murderer will, perversely, give the reader far more pleasure than having him find out that it was the detestable brother. Would Jekyll and Hyde have made as compelling a story if Jekyll hadn't been a likable, respectable doctor?

The modern writer of crime stories has a wide range of choice. A story may be a whodunit puzzle, a whydunit psychological tale, a comedy, a spy story, or it may not fit any category at all. For many readers, the attraction of crime fiction is that the stories have beginnings, middles, and ends and, as a rule, coherent plots. A crime novel without at least one murder is almost unthinkable. It would have to be outstanding to get by an editor, and then, very likely, it wouldn't be published as a mystery. With short stories, it's different: A large proportion of them don't have murders, and frequently the crime is relatively trivial, or hardly a crime at all.

19

WHAT IF . . .?
by *William G. Tapply*

"WHERE DO YOU GET YOUR IDEAS?" It's the question fiction writers are most often asked.

Typically, we reply, "Why, ideas are everywhere. The newspapers. Television. Cocktail party conversation. Dreams. The problem isn't finding ideas. The problem is recognizing those that are useful, those that can be converted into a story, and then knowing what to do with them." The proper answer to the question, however, is, "Ideas come from inside my head. If you want a story idea, that's where you have to look."

Brady Coyne, the lawyer-sleuth hero of my mystery series, ponders difficult cases from the banks of a trout stream or the little balcony of his waterfront apartment in Boston. The process is identical to what I as his creator go through trying to think up adventures for him. Brady describes this in *Dead Winter:*

> I drank and smoked and thought. The breeze came at me from the sea, moist and organic. The bell buoy out there clanged its mournful rhythm. From behind me came the muffled city noises—the wheeze of traffic through the nighttime streets, the occasional punctuation of siren and horn, the almost subsonic hum and murmur of dense human life.
>
> I remembered the Vermont woods, and my picnic with Kat, and how the birds and bugs and animals and river sounded, and

how the pine forest smelled, and how my rainbow trout never missed his mayfly.

And while one part of my mind registered all of these surface things and wandered freely on its own associations, a different part of it looked for pattern and purpose in three North Shore murders, and a third part watched what was going on and tried not to judge it or guide it.

That's how a writer thinks up a story idea. It's a process of disciplined free association. Learning how to do it has not been easy, and doing it is very hard work.

I have never thought of a useful idea unless I have been obsessed with the need for one. A good idea has never come to me when I wasn't looking for it.

The layman's vision of the fiction writer is someone brimming with ideas that demand being converted into words. But for those of us who have committed ourselves to produce novels more or less regularly, it's not the idea that motivates the writing of the book. Rather, it's the commitment, whether contractual or personal, to write a book that motivates the quest for an idea.

An idea isn't a story, and a story isn't a novel. An idea is a flame that ignites the individual creative imagination. It can usually be stated in a simple declarative statement. For example, "A teacher discovers that one of his colleagues is in fact a fugitive from justice living under a false identity." Or, "The owner of a million-dollar rare stamp, thought to be the only one of its kind in existence, is contacted by someone who claims to possess a duplicate of that stamp." Or, again, "The dead man found frozen in a Boston alley, first assumed to be a homeless bum, turns out to be the nephew of an influential Massachusetts politician."

What is a red-hot idea for me will be a dead ember for another writer. An idea sets off a complicated chain reaction, a sequence of imagined events that the writer transforms into scenes populated by imaginary people. That is a story. When the writer puts it all onto paper, it becomes a novel.

Look for the spark that ignites an idea. It is, in fact, true that writers do go to places to seek that spark. Mary Higgins Clark sits in courtrooms, hoping to hear or see something that will inspire one of her complex psychological mystery novels. Some mystery fiction writers hang around with newspaper reporters or lurk in barrooms; others ride with policemen. All of them read compulsively and eclectically. Then they exercise that discipline of controlled free association.

Sparks plus imagination

Sparks are indeed everywhere. The ideas they kindle grow from the writer's imagination.

The "idea" for my first novel, *Death at Charity's Point,* was sparked by the televised news story of a fugitive from the law, who, after several years of living quietly under an assumed identity, a pillar of his little rural community, decided to turn himself in. At the time I heard this story, I had decided to write a novel. Lacking an idea, I had learned intuitively to treat every stimulus from my environment as this potential spark for a novel.

"What if," I asked myself, someone in this fugitive's little community had uncovered his true identity? And *what if* he didn't want to be brought to justice? Might he commit murder to protect his secret?

My mind raced with possibilities. I sketched out scenarios. A dead body, a fictional community. Clues and red herrings. Characters and places. And, not to diminish the difficulty of it, the spark evolved into a story, and the story finally became a novel.

That news item was broadcast nationally. It appeared in newspapers across the country. Millions of Americans heard it or read it. But, as far as I know, it sparked the idea for a novel *only for me*. It worked for me because I was at that time vigorously engaged in the hard task of *seeking* an idea, and because it merged with that unique entity that is my imagination—the product of my peculiar history, personality, and life experiences. And if it had happened to inspire someone else, the product would certainly have been unrecognizably different from mine.

When I completed my first novel, I wanted desperately to write another one. Constantly on the alert for an idea, I came across an item in the "Ask the [Boston] Globe" column, responding to the question, "What is the most valuable postage stamp in the world?" The one-of-a-kind British Guyana black and magenta, was the answer. It brought $850,000 at auction in 1980, its extraordinary value attributed to its uniqueness.

What if someone should discover a duplicate of this stamp? What would it do to the value of the original one, and what might the owner of the original do to acquire the alleged "duplicate"? There were motives for murder there, I decided, and the crude shape of a plot began to materialize as I thought about it.

To stimulate my imagination, I began to read about philately and stories of rare, old stamps. I sought out stamp dealers and listened to their tales. I asked about forgeries and fakes and stamp auctions. This research gave me information that would lend verisimilitude to my story. At the same time, it fired my imagination, suggesting characters, subplots, conflicts, and motivations for crime.

The "Ask the Globe" column was not the idea for my book. But it sparked the idea that evolved into *The Dutch Blue Error,* my second novel.

Several winters ago, a *Boston Globe* columnist wrote about a discovery of the frozen body of an anonymous, presumably homeless man in the car yards of South Boston. The man had died of electrocution when he urinated on the third rail. I thought that item might spark a story for me, and

I clipped it out. I even invented a title, imagining that dead man had been clothed in second-hand military garb: *The Marine Corpse*.

I had the spark and the title, but I didn't have an idea. I tried asking myself *What if* the dead man had been murdered? *What if* . . . but it didn't work. Hours of free association produced only frustration.

I went to the library and checked out all the books I could find on the homeless. One of them was written by a young sociology professor who grew a beard and rode the rails for a year, living among the hoboes to gather his data.

What if the dead man in my story was such a man, not really a bum, but a researcher in disguise who had inadvertently stumbled onto something criminal? A theft? Drug dealing? An international political plot? What about the personal life of this dead man? Might he have been one of Brady's clients? The nephew of a state senator, perhaps, and a homosexual whose secret might scandalize his family.

Thus was born *The Marine Corpse,* Brady's fourth case.

Sometimes it takes two sparks to ignite the flame of an idea.

The chance remark by a baseball announcer about a prematurely retired big-league pitcher failed to set off the chain of "what if" questions that became a novel until I read a newspaper account of a manhunt for a divorced man who had allegedly kidnapped his son. *What if* that pitcher's son was kidnapped? *What if* the reason for his retirement was linked to the kidnapping?

A week of salmon fishing in Maine wilderness suggested an offbeat setting for murder, but no idea emerged until a friend complained to me about a lawsuit filed by the Penobscot Indians that might result in his losing his summer cottage. *What if,* I thought, an old Indian guide worked at a remote Maine fishing lodge? *What if* one of the guests was murdered, and the Indian was wrongly accused?

My long-standing fascination with local politics seemed

to lead me nowhere, until I read an article on crack, that deadly, most addictive form of cocaine that was being widely distributed in small towns. *What if* the son of an ambitious politician was wrongly accused of drug dealing and murder?

Synergy and serendipity

In each of these cases, a single spark was not enough. But when I found the second spark and brought the two together, an idea burst into flame. Serendipity! That seemed to me to explain the way ideas emerge, but only after hard thinking that may look like daydreaming and seems to come unexpectedly. But it is no accident.

Learning to ask those "what if" and "then what" and "what next" questions; to experiment by linking two or more apparently unrelated premises; to follow my imagination as it wonders and supposes; to know when it is leading somewhere, and to shut it off when it is not—that's what is necessary, and it's not easy. It's not always even fun. But it's how I think up my ideas.

"You must be bubbling with ideas," my friends tell me, "to write so many books, one after the other."

If they only knew.

20 SERIES CHARACTERS IN MYSTERY FICTION
by *Michael Underwood*

IT'S A SAFE GENERALIZATION that publishers prefer mysteries to have a continuing character. One has to look no further than Hercule Poirot, Lord Peter Wimsey, Perry Mason and Philip Marlowe, never forgetting James Bond, to perceive the truth of this. Although the inspired creators of that particular lot are now all dead, their creations live on to beguile new readers and have been joined by protagonists likely to prove just as durable: H. R. F. Keating's Inspector Ghote of The Bombay Police, P.D. James's Commander Dalgleish, Ruth Rendell's Chief Inspector Wexford and perhaps most original of them all, Ellis Peters' Brother Cadfael, a 12th-century monk.

Reader identification remains the name of the game. Readers of crime novels want familiarity. And who better to provide that than a Miss Marple or a Nero Wolfe? If, therefore, you are thinking of writing a mystery, I suggest that you create a protagonist who will win your readers and send them looking for your next book.

What does this mean to the author? With luck he will be financially rewarded, though he is also likely to suffer spells of frustration and to harbor homicidal thoughts toward his creation. Nicholas Freeling actually killed off the popular police detective Van der Valk and has never been forgiven by many of his faithful readers.

133

A number of writers intersperse their series mystery novels with others. Ruth Rendell has her Chief Inspector Wexford books, but also writes non-Wexford crime stories under her own name or as Barbara Vine. And Simon Brett from time to time gives his alcoholic actor-detective Charles Paris a rest and comes up with excellent non-Paris mysteries.

Nevertheless, it is my guess that an author's steadfast fans do not want a familiar protagonist to remain absent for too long, otherwise they too may desert. Readers aren't especially noted for their sentimentality.

Wanted: A plausible investigator

How does a writer set about creating an interesting series character? Obviously, there are no set rules. To me it's important that that character is plausibly able to undertake the role of an investigator. I doubt whether today's readers would easily accept the sort of gifted amateur of yesteryear who was always conveniently on hand to give the professional police the benefit of his advice in their bumbling efforts to solve a murder. The delight of Miss Marple is, of course, her period flavor. Admittedly, the modern "private eye" is still very much around (more so in the States than in England), but it would be a nice change to meet one who is non-smoking, non-drinking, and even has a happy family life. But maybe this is too eccentric a conception.

Coming to my own experience, I have written over forty mystery novels. The early ones had the same Scotland Yard detective as the protagonist. But he was a somewhat colorless figure, and nobody mourned his eventual fade-out. He retired to the limbo that claims most fictional characters. Later, I wrote a number of books in which a detective sergeant and his wife (an ex-police officer herself) appeared in tandem as protagonists. But they never really caught on and were quietly dropped to no one's regret. It was my British editor who observed that part of the trouble was that the wife was so much brighter than her husband. Maybe their roles should have been reversed with her staying on in the police force and him looking after the kids at home.

You may well be wondering how I've managed to keep going without (until relatively recently) having a satisfactory series character. The answer is that all my books have had a strong legal background, with court scenes and the like, which provided them with their own particular hallmark. But now I seem to have created a character with more enduring qualities than her predecessors. She is Rosa Epton, a British solicitor who has made her modest mark in the series of novels in which she has appeared. My feelings toward her are ambivalent, but she seems here to stay—at least for the time being. Her creation has aroused a certain amount of popular interest, and I have been asked more than once how I, a male, came to create a female protagonist. Was I sociologically motivated? The answer is less worthy than that and reflects little credit on me. Rosa Epton first appeared as a lawyer's clerk in a novel called *A Pinch of Snuff* (published in 1974). She played only a small part, and when the book was finished, she joined the rest of the characters in the limbo reserved for those who make one-time appearances in books. It was not till several years later that my lively and stimulating American editor wrote to me and said, in effect, "You often create good characters in your books, but then they vanish, never to be heard of again, e.g. Rosa Epton in *A Pinch of Snuff.* I'm sure you could build her up into a series character. . . ."

After I had reminded myself who she was, I decided to do as he had suggested and thus she has appeared in the last ten books I've written.

In England, the law is still a considerably hidebound profession in which convention prevails and pomposity is not unknown. I knew, however, that if Rosa was to survive, she mustn't be bound by convention, even though she was proud to be a lawyer. I felt also that I had to guard against

her becoming a "bossy-boots," which is another professional hazard. To this end, she now has the status of junior
partner in a London firm of solicitors, her senior partner
being an older and more experienced person who, in fact,
gave her the chance to become a solicitor. She has in my
most recent novels acquired a Hong Kong Chinese boy-
friend who is also a solicitor, but with an international
clientele. I hope that she has grown into an identifiable and
interesting character with a minimum of irritating habits.
I'm aware that she grates on some of my readers, though the
majority seem to approve of her. For the present, our fates
are linked. Like other series characters in mystery fiction,
she doesn't age as rapidly as her creator, say one year for
every five of his. I now know exactly what she looks like,
though her appearance in my mind's eye used to become
disconcertingly unfocused when I first began writing about
her.

I think the principal pitfall for the author using a continuing character is probably staleness. If a writer becomes
bored with his or her character, it will soon be apparent to
the reader. It is known that Agatha Christie wearied of
Poirot long before his eventual demise, but she was, so to
speak, tethered to him by chains of gold. I suspect that a
good many authors of mystery novels at times entertain
homicidal thoughts toward their protagonists. Anyway, have
fun deciding on your own series characters. There's still
unlimited scope for an original creation, and mystery readers (bless them!) remain an enduring legion.

21 SUSPENSE: HOW TO KEEP THOSE PAGES TURNING
by *Phyllis A. Whitney*

WHAT IS GOING TO HAPPEN NEXT?

That is the question I most want my readers to ask, because it tells me I've kept them turning the pages of my novel. Page-turning is no happenstance matter: Every phase of a novel—mine or yours—must deal with holding the reader's attention, and this means being aware of the techniques that build suspense.

Small problems and small emotions never carry us far. I must ask myself early in my planning what every character wants—*desperately*. The "wants" of different characters are going to clash, and if they are strong, powerful drives, I'll have the beginnings of a page-turner.

Each of my characters must have a secret—something they don't want known, which will affect the progress of the story, as what is hidden is gradually revealed. When I consider these hidden motives, my imagination is fired into inventing interesting action. I remember one young writer who told me that her imagination sometimes seemed like a desert, with nothing growing there. But deserts can flourish with life when the right seeds are planted.

Of course, it is vitally necessary for readers to care what happens to my main character. Terrible disasters will befall her (I name them to myself ahead of time) if she doesn't win out, and rich rewards await her if she does. This should be obvious, but sometimes we don't think ahead, and our stories turn weak and flabby.

Human, imperfect—but sympathetic

Sympathy for the main character is paramount in this type of fiction, and sometimes I get into trouble on this score. The critics I trust to read my manuscript before submission may say, "But this character is too self-centered. I don't like her. She's inconsiderate and pushy." *I* didn't see her that way. There can be a glow of illusion between my eyes and my typed words that can keep me from seeing exactly what I've written. Of course, as soon as this is pointed out, the rosy glow is gone, and I can see the flaws and correct them. Main characters must be human and imperfect, but they must remain sympathetic. Too often I start to read a novel in which I care about none of the characters—what happens to them doesn't seem to matter, since there's no one I want to see win. So I stop reading.

In contrast to an appealing heroine, there must be an evildoer who makes a powerful villain. In a mystery novel, we may not be sure who this villain is, and since all the other characters have their own cross-purposes and are busy muddying the waters (because of all those secrets), I can manage to fool the reader most of the time. Readers like to be fooled. When they guess what I'm up to and aren't surprised, they're disappointed.

Emotion is one of the important qualities we must work for to hold our readers' attention. Caring and feeling are tied together, and every part of a story (long or short) conveys an emotional message, whether we are aware of it or not. So we'd better convey the right emotion. When we handle this aspect well, our readers will be touched, alarmed, delighted, despairing, anxious—deeply involved—and they won't put the book down.

Tantalize your reader

We must please at times, as well as alarm, since discouragement that lasts too long can cause a loss of interest. *(This is too depressing—I don't want to read it.)* But whether the scene is quiet and happy, or one in which everything is going wrong, we must tantalize, promise, throw out hints for the future. (Dear reader, you only *think* you know what's going to happen—just wait!)

When I was in the early planning stages of *Flaming Tree,* I knew only that my setting would be Carmel, California, and that a nine-year-old boy who has been brain-injured in a terrible fall would feature in the story. The first question I faced was how to tie my heroine into this situation, and I began slowly to form the bricks that would build a strong understructure. My heroine is a physical therapist who works with children. She has recently suffered the loss of her own small son in a driving accident that may have been her fault. As a result, she has been estranged from her husband and divorced. She goes to Carmel to visit an aunt and to recuperate emotionally. The stage is set for her involvement in what is about to happen.

In Carmel, she is asked as a therapist to see the injured boy. His father has been told by doctors that his son will never be anything but a vegetable, and he is about to give up. The child's mother was injured at the same time and doesn't seem to care about her son. The boy is to be sent to an institution where hopeless cases are cared for. My heroine visits the child in his parents' house, has reason to think that in spite of what everyone believes, some intelligence exists in him. She stays to fight the father for the little boy's life, and the situation is already emotion-fraught.

For at least two months before I started to write anything, I began to ask myself questions. (Why does the mother *not* want her son to recover?) I always keep lists of such questions (important and minor) and write them down on slips of paper I keep on hand when I'm at work. I write answers in my notebook as they come to me and cross out the answered questions, making space for new ones. This process goes on almost until I am at the end of the book.

Another good way to create interest is to use "things" when writing your story. Every scene happens in a physical world, and exciting action and plot development can grow out of the objects you plant in your scenes. In *Flaming Tree,* a woman in a painting is wearing a string of wooden beads from Africa. When I first mentioned the beads, they were merely a bit of description. But I watch for such usable items, and develop a purpose for them if they show promise. A bead from this strand appears on someone's desk, and there is a mystery about it. I didn't know this was going to happen but decided to use the idea of the broken strand in future action. Since the "things" one uses should be interesting in themselves, I "carved" ugly little faces on each bead. Eventually, it was revealed how the strand was broken, and the beads became an integral part of the plot.

Unexpected happenings, as well as physical items, can be picked up and used later to develop interest. There is a scene in *Flaming Tree* in which the small boy is taken on an outing in his wheelchair. The father is a little more hopeful and ready to go along with what my main character wants to attempt. Then something occurs that sends the boy into a state of gasping terror, and the father renews his opposition to the heroine's plans, blaming her. What frightened the boy proved very useful to me, though I didn't know that was going to happen, and of course it is revealed by the end of the story. Tantalize. Don't tell everything you know!

I watch for that flash of inventiveness that can come when I am writing a scene. Some of the best bits in my novels are happenings that surprise *me*.

The time element in fiction can be used to build strong suspense. In *Flaming Tree,* the boy's father gives my heroine one week to prove that the boy isn't a "vegetable." So she is up against an almost impossible challenge from the first. Pages turn because the pressure of time is on.

Don't start writing too soon. This is the common disease of the young writer. It is one I had to recover from too—that eagerness to get it down on paper. The vision seems so wonderful, the urgency to transfer it all into words is so strong, that we can't wait. And we start pouring it out on paper. We work in a state of high excitement for several pages, even for a chapter or two. And then the impulse dies, because we don't really know where we're going and our writing begins to founder.

Fortunately, this isn't fatal. We'll do it better next time around, when we've found our true direction. We may even save some of what we've written with such enthusiasm, but the time always comes when *thinking* is necessary. Instead of treading water aimlessly, we can then swim toward a shore we can see.

During the actual writing, I try not to think about the techniques discussed in this article. That comes before and after. I am simply there in my story—not exactly taking part, but certainly on the scene watching it happen. People have asked me if I become my heroine. I don't think so—I believe I am the watcher-in-the-shadows, simply recording what I see and feel. I must allow my right brain its free, creative flow without any distracting criticism from that practical left brain.

People have also asked me whom I write for. The answer is easy—only myself. While writing, I am totally unaware of readers. There isn't anyone but my characters on the scene while I'm at my typewriter. If I am sufficiently involved, then all I need to do is allow the actions and the people to come to life. If I do this well enough (having thought it through ahead of time), readers out there will be turning my pages.

22

A LAYMAN'S GUIDE TO LAW
AND THE COURTS

WRITERS of suspense and mystery fiction will find the following information a valuable reference tool for use in describing points of law, courtroom procedures, criminal actions, legal transactions, and arrest procedures. This is a condensation of *Law and the Courts,* prepared by the American Bar Association.—*Ed.*

The processes of the law and the courts are baffling and mysterious to many laymen. The following material traces the steps normally involved in a civil case and in a criminal case, explaining the procedures common to most of them. It was prepared for use by nonlawyers (writers and others). The Standing Committee on Association Communications of the American Bar Association will, upon request, be pleased to offer assistance to writers in reviewing articles, scripts, and other material, for accuracy in legal procedure. The ABA Public Information Department also will be glad to help answer questions or direct inquiries to knowledgeable sources.

Some variations of procedure exist among the various state courts, and among the federal courts as well. When the occasion requires, details of procedure in particular courts, or in special

This chapter is a condensation of *Law and the Courts:* A Layman's Handbook of Court Procedures, and is reprinted by permission of the American Bar Association. The complete booklet is available for 50¢ from the American Bar Association, Circulation Department, 750 North Lake Shore Drive, Chicago, IL 60611. Copyright © 1974 by American Bar Association.

types of litigation, can be supplied by local attorneys, by court public information officers or other court officials.

Criminal cases

BRINGING THE CHARGE. Criminal charges are instituted against an individual in one of two ways:

1) Through an *indictment,* or *true bill,* voted by a grand jury, or

2) Through the filing of an *information* in court by the prosecuting attorney (sometimes called the county, district or state's attorney), alleging the commission of a crime.

In either case, the charge must set forth the time, date and place of the alleged criminal act as well as the nature of the charge.

In most states, crimes of a serious nature, such as murder or treason, may be charged by indictment only. In some states, the prosecutor has the option in any case to proceed by way of indictment or information.

THE GRAND JURY. The grand jury is a body of citizens (usually 16, but varying in number from state to state) summoned by the court to inquire into crimes committed in the county or, in the case of federal grand juries, in the federal court district.

Grand jury proceedings are private and secret. Prospective defendants are not entitled to be present at the proceedings, and no one appears to cross-examine witnesses on the defendants' behalf.

However, a witness before a federal grand jury is free to describe his testimony to anyone he pleases, after he leaves the grand jury room. To this extent, such proceedings are not secret.

Although all states have provision for impaneling a grand jury, only about half use it as a regular arm of law enforcement. In the others, the prosecutor, on his own responsibility, is empowered to make formal accusation of all, or of all but the most serious, crimes.

In states where the grand jury is utilized, it is convened at regular intervals, or it may be impaneled at special times by the court to consider important cases.

The grand jury has broad investigative powers: it may compel the attendance of witnesses; require the taking of oaths, and compel answers to questions and the submission of records.

Ordinarily, however, the grand jury hears such witnesses as the prosecutor calls before it and considers only the cases presented to it by the prosecutor.

Nevertheless, a grand jury may undertake inquiries of its own, in effect taking the initiative away from the prosecutor. In common parlance, this is known as a "runaway" grand jury.

The grand jury's traditional function is to determine whether information elicited by the prosecutor, or by its own inquiries, is adequate to warrant the return of an indictment or true bill charging a person or persons with a particular crime. If the grand jury concludes that the evidence does not warrant a formal charge, it may return a *no bill*.

In several states, powers of investigation similar to those of the grand jury are conferred by law upon a single person, a judicial officer or a deputy appointed by him, known as a "one man grand jury."

ARREST PROCEDURE. When an indictment is returned by a grand jury, or an information is filed by the prosecuting attorney, the clerk of the court issues a *warrant* for the arrest of the person charged, if he has not already been arrested and taken into custody.

The law usually requires in a *felony* case (generally, a crime for which a person may be confined in the penitentiary) that the defendant must promptly be brought before a magistrate or justice of the peace (in federal cases, the U.S. Commissioner) and be permitted to post bond, in order to secure release from custody, and either request or waive a *preliminary hearing*. When the grand jury indicts, there is no preliminary hearing. In most states, however, persons charged with murder are not eligible for release on a bail bond.

Many jurisdictions permit law enforcement officials to hold a person without formal charge up to 24 hours for the purpose of investigation. But he may not be held for an unreasonable time unless a criminal charge is filed. In addition, the defendant formally charged with a crime is entitled to an attorney at all times. If he is unable to procure an attorney and if he requests counsel, the court will appoint an attorney to represent him, at public expense and without cost to him.

Special Note

Under the so-called Miranda decision of the United States Supreme Court, the following "basic Miranda procedure" and "typical Miranda statement given by an officer" are used:

I.   Typical Miranda statement given by officer

Before we ask you any questions, you must understand what your rights are.

You have the right to remain silent. You are not required to say anything to us at any time or to answer any questions. Anything you say can and will be used against you in court.

You have the right to talk to a lawyer for advice before we question you and to have him with you during questioning.

If you cannot afford a lawyer and want one, a lawyer will be provided for you free of charge.

If you want to answer questions now without a lawyer present, you will still have the right to stop answering at any time. You also have the right to stop answering at any time until you talk to a lawyer.

II.   Basic Miranda procedure

1.   Warnings given *before* questioning a suspect who is *in custody* (custody = focus of interrogation + not permitted to move on).

2.   Warnings always given when—
    a.   subject is placed under *arrest.*
    b.   interrogation in police *presence,* i.e., in station, or in squad car.
    c.   if it is clear to officer that suspect thinks he has to answer.

3.   Warnings not necessary for a mere witness (even grand jury witness who is not yet focus of investigation).

4.   Warnings should be repeated after delay in questioning. Warning should be repeated when questioning officer changes.

5. Officer should immediately *stop* questions when suspect becomes silent *or* requests lawyer. If suspect agrees to talk and then goes silent, questions should stop.

6. Officer should give warning even to suspect who claims to make a statement that will show his innocence.

PRELIMINARY HEARING. If the individual charged with a crime requests a preliminary hearing before a magistrate, the court will set a hearing within a reasonably short time. At the hearing, the state must present sufficient evidence to convince the magistrate that there is reason to believe the defendant has committed the crime with which he is charged. The defendant must be present at this hearing, and he may or may not present evidence on his own behalf.

If the magistrate believes the evidence justifies it, he will order the defendant *bound over* for trial in the proper court—that is, placed under bond for appearance at trial, or held in jail if the charge involved is not a bailable offense or if the defendant is unable to post bond. The magistrate also may decide that even without bond the accused will most likely appear in court for his trial and therefore will release him on his *own recognizance,* that is, on his own promise to appear. If he concludes the state has failed to produce sufficient evidence in the preliminary hearing, the magistrate may dismiss the charge and order the defendant released.

ARRAIGNMENT. In most instances, a criminal case is placed on the court's calendar for *arraignment.* On the date fixed, the accused appears, the indictment or information is read to him, his rights are explained by the judge, and he is asked whether he pleads *guilty* or *not guilty* to the charge.

If he pleads not guilty, his case will be set later for trial; if he pleads guilty, his case ordinarily will be set later for sentencing. In cases of minor offenses, sentences may be imposed immediately. But in some states, arraignment and plea are separate proceedings, held on different days.

PREPARATION FOR TRIAL. As in civil cases, very careful preparation on the part of the state and the defense precedes the trial.

However, the defense may first enter a motion challenging the jurisdiction of the court over the particular offense involved, or over the particular defendant. The defense attorney also may file a *demurrer,* or motion for dismissal, as in a civil suit.

In preparing for trial, attorneys for both sides will interview prospective witnesses and, if deemed necessary, secure expert evidence, and gather testimony concerning ballistics, chemical tests, casts and other similar data.

Trials: civil or criminal

While in detail there are minor differences in trial procedure between civil and criminal cases, the basic pattern in the courtroom is the same. Consequently, this section treats the trial steps collectively.

OFFICERS OF THE COURT. The *judge* is the officer who is either elected or appointed to preside over the court. If the case is tried before a jury, the judge rules upon points of law dealing with trial procedure, presentation of the evidence and the law of the case. If the case is tried before the judge alone, he will determine the facts in addition to performing the aforementioned duties.

The *court clerk* is an officer of the court, also either elected or appointed, who at the beginning of the trial, upon the judge's instruction, gives the entire panel of prospective jurors (*veniremen*) an oath. By this oath, the venireman promises that, if called, he will truly answer any question concerning his qualifications to sit as a juror in the case.

Any venireman who is disqualified by law, or has a valid reason to be excused under the law, ordinarily is excused by the judge at this time. A person may be disqualified from jury duty because he is not a resident voter or householder, because of age, hearing defects, or because he has served recently on a jury.

Then the court clerk will draw names of the remaining veniremen from a box, and they will take seats in the jury box. After twelve veniremen have been approved as jurors by the judge and the attorneys, the court clerk will administer an oath to the persons so chosen "to well and truly try the cause."

The *bailiff* is an officer of the court whose duties are to keep order in the courtroom, to call witnesses, and to take charge of the jury as instructed by the court at such times as the jury may not be in the courtroom, and particularly when, having received the case, the jury is deliberating upon its decision. It is the duty of the bailiff to see that no one talks with or attempts to influence the jurors in any manner.

The *court reporter* has the duty of recording all proceedings in the courtroom, and listing and marking for identification any exhibits offered or introduced into evidence. In some states, the clerk of the court has charge of exhibits.

The *attorneys* are officers of the court whose duties are to represent their respective clients and present the evidence on their behalf.

The role of the attorney is sometimes misunderstood, particularly in criminal proceedings. Our system of criminal jurisprudence presumes every defendant to be innocent until proved guilty beyond a *reasonable doubt.* Every defendant is entitled to be represented by legal counsel, regardless of the unpopularity of his cause. This is a constitutional safeguard.

It is entirely ethical for an attorney to represent a defendant whom the community may assume to be guilty. The accused is entitled to counsel in order that he be protected from conviction on insufficient evidence, and he is entitled to every protection which the law affords.

JURY LIST. The trial jury in either a civil or criminal case is called a *petit jury.* It is chosen by lot by the court clerk from a previously compiled list called a *venire,* or in some places the *jury array.*

Many persons are exempted from jury duty by reason of their occupations. These exemptions differ from state to state, but in some jurisdictions those automatically exempted include lawyers, physicians, dentists, pharmacists, teachers and clergymen. In a number of others, nurses, journalists, printers, railroad, telephone and telegraph employees, government officials, firemen and policemen are among the exempt occupational groups.

On occasion, the qualification of all the jurors may be challenged. This is called a *challenge to the array* and generally is based on the allegation that the officers charged with selecting the jurors did so in an illegal manner.

SELECTING THE JURY. In most cases, a jury of twelve is required in either a civil or criminal proceeding. In some courts, alternate jurors are selected to take the places of members of the regular panel who may become disabled during the trial. These alternate jurors hear the evidence just as do the regular jurors, but do not participate in the deliberations unless a regular juror or jurors become disabled.

The jury selection begins with the calling by the court clerk of twelve veniremen whose names are selected at random from a box, to take their places in the jury enclosure. The attorneys for the parties, or sometimes the judge, may then make a brief statement of the facts involved, for the purpose of acquainting the jurors with sufficient facts so that they may intelligently answer the questions put to them by the judge and the attorneys. The questions elicit information such as the name, the occupation, the place of business and residence of the prospective juror, and any personal knowledge he may have of the case. This questioning of the jurors is known as the *voir dire*.

If the venireman expresses an opinion or prejudice which will affect his judgment in the case, the court will dismiss him for *cause,* and a substitute juror will be called by the court clerk. There is no limit on the number of jurors who may be excused *for cause.*

In addition to the challenges for cause, each party has the right to exercise a specific number of *peremptory challenges.* This permits an attorney to excuse a particular juror without having to state a cause. If a peremptory challenge is exercised, another juror then is called until attorneys on both sides have exercised all of the peremptory challenges permitted by law, or they have waived further challenges. The number of peremptory challenges is limited and varies with the type of case.

The jury is then sworn in by the court clerk to try the case. The remaining members of the jury panel are excused and directed to report at a future date when another case will be called, or excused and directed to report to another court in session at the time.

SEPARATING THE WITNESSES. In certain cases, civil or criminal, the attorney on either side may advise the court that he is *calling for the rule* on witnesses. This means that, except for the plaintiff or complaining witness and the defendant, all witnesses who may testify for either party will be excluded from the courtroom until they are called to testify. These witnesses are admonished by the judge not to discuss the case or their testimony with other witnesses or persons, except the attorneys. This is sometimes called a *separation of witnesses*. If the rule is not called for, the witnesses may remain in the courtroom if they desire.

OPENING STATEMENTS. After selection of the jury, the plaintiff's attorney, or attorney for the state in a criminal case, may make an opening statement to advise the jury what he intends to prove in the case. This statement must be confined to facts intended to be elicited in evidence and cannot be argumentative. The attorney for the defendant also may make an opening statement for the same purpose or, in some states, may reserve the opening statement until the end of the plaintiff's or state's case. Either party may waive his opening statement if he desires.

PRESENTATION OF EVIDENCE. The plaintiff in a civil case, or the state in a criminal case, will begin the presentation of evidence with their *witnesses*. These usually will include the plaintiff in a civil case or complaining witness in a criminal case, although they are not required to testify.

A witness may testify to a matter of fact. He can tell what he saw, heard (unless it is hearsay as explained below), felt, smelled or touched through the use of his physical senses.

A witness also may be used to identify documents, pictures or other physical exhibits in the trial.

Generally, he cannot state his opinion or give his conclusion unless he is an expert or especially qualified to do so. In some instances, a witness may be permitted to express an opinion, for example, as to the speed an auto was traveling or whether a person was intoxicated.

A witness who has been qualified in a particular field as an *expert* may give his opinion based upon the facts in evidence and may state the reasons for that opinion. Sometimes the facts in evidence are put to the expert in a question called a *hypothetical question*. The question assumes the truth of the facts contained in it. Other times, an expert is asked to state an opinion based on personal knowledge of the facts through his own examination or investigation.

Generally, a witness cannot testify to *hearsay*, that is, what someone else has told him outside the presence of the parties to the action.

Also, a witness is not permitted to testify about matters that are too remote to have any bearing on the decision of the case, or matters that are irrelevant or immaterial.

Usually, an attorney may not ask *leading questions* of his own witness, although an attorney is sometimes allowed to elicit routine, noncontroversial information. A leading question is one which suggests the answer desired.

Objections may be made by the opposing counsel to leading questions, or to questions that call for an opinion or conclusion on the part of the witness, or require an answer based on hearsay. There are many other reasons for objections under the rules of evidence.

Objections are often made in the following form: "I object to that question on the ground that it is irrelevant and immaterial and for the further reason that it calls for an opinion and conclusion of the witness." Many jurisdictions require that the objection specify why the question is not proper. The judge will thereupon sustain or deny the objection. If sustained, another question must then be asked, or the same question be rephrased in proper form.

If an objection to a question is sustained on either direct or cross-examination, the attorney asking the question may make an *offer to prove*. This offer is dictated to the court reporter away from the hearing of the jury. In it, the attorney states the answer which the witness would have given if permitted. The offer forms part of the record if the case is subsequently appealed.

If the objection is overruled, the witness may then answer. The attorney who made the objection may thereupon take an *exception*, which simply means that he is preserving a record so that, if the case is appealed, he may argue that the court erred in overruling the objection. In some states, the rules permit an automatic exception to an adverse ruling without its being asked for in each instance.

CROSS-EXAMINATION. When plaintiff's attorney or the state's attorney has finished his direct examination of the witness, the defendant's attorney or opposing counsel may then cross-examine the witness on any matter about which the witness has been questioned initially in direct examination. The cross-examining attorney may ask leading questions for the purpose of inducing the witness to testify about matters which he may otherwise have chosen to ignore.

On cross-examination, the attorney may try to bring out prejudice or bias of the witness, such as his relationship or friendship to the party, or other interest in the case. The witness can be asked if he has been convicted of a felony or crime involving moral turpitude, since this bears upon his credibility.

The plaintiff's attorney may object to certain questions asked on cross-examination on previously mentioned grounds or because they deal with facts not touched upon in direct examination.

RE-DIRECT EXAMINATION. After the opposing attorney is finished with his cross-examination, the attorney who called the witness has the right to ask questions on *re-direct examination*. The re-direct examination covers new matters brought out on cross-examination and generally is an effort to rehabilitate a witness whose testimony on direct examination has been weakened by cross-examination.

Then the opposing attorney may re-cross-examine.

DEMURRER TO PLAINTIFF'S OR STATE'S CASE, OR MOTION FOR DIRECTED VERDICT. At the conclusion of the plaintiff's or state's evidence, the attorney will announce that the plaintiff or state *rests*.

Then, away from the presence of the jury, the defendant's counsel may demur to the plaintiff's or state's case on the ground that a cause of action or that the commission of a crime has not been proven. In many states, this is known as a *motion for a direct verdict,* that is, a verdict which the judge orders the jury to return.

The judge will either sustain or overrule the demurrer or motion. If it is sustained, the case is concluded. If it is overruled, the defendant then is given the opportunity to present his evidence.

PRESENTATION OF EVIDENCE BY THE DEFENDANT. The defense attorney may elect to present no evidence, or he may present certain evidence but not place the defendant upon the stand.

In a criminal case, the defendant need not take the stand unless he wishes to do so. The defendant has constitutional protection against self-incrimination. He is not required to prove his innocence. The plaintiff or the state has the *burden of proof*.

In a civil case, the plaintiff must prove his case by a *preponderance of the evidence*. This means the greater weight of the evidence.

In a criminal case, the evidence of guilt must be *beyond a reasonable doubt*.

The defendant is presumed to be not negligent or liable in a civil case, and not guilty in a criminal case.

The defense attorney may feel that the burden of proof has not been sustained, or that presentation of the defendant's witnesses might strengthen the plaintiff's case. If the defendant does present evidence, he does so in the same manner as the plaintiff or the state, as described above, and the plaintiff or state will cross-examine the defendant's witnesses.

REBUTTAL EVIDENCE. At the conclusion of the defendant's case, the plaintiff or state's attorney may then present rebuttal witnesses or evidence designed to refute the testimony and evidence presented by the defendant. The matter covered is evidence on which the plaintiff or state did not present evidence in its *case in chief* initially; or it may be a new witness to contradict the defendant's witness. If there is a so-called *surprise witness*, this is often where you will find him.

After rebuttal evidence, the defendant may present additional evidence to contradict it.

FINAL MOTIONS. At the conclusion of all the evidence, the defendant may again renew his demurrer or motion for directed verdict.

The motion is made away from the presence of the jury. If the demurrer or motion is sustained, the case is concluded. If overruled, the trial proceeds.

Thus, the case has now been concluded on the evidence, and it is ready to be submitted to the jury.

CONFERENCES DURING THE TRIAL. Occasionally during the trial, the lawyers will ask permission to approach the bench and speak to the judge, or the judge may call them to the bench. They whisper about admissibility of certain evidence, irregularities in the trial or other matters. The judge and lawyers speak in inaudible tones because the jurors might be prejudiced by what they hear. The question of admissibility of evidence is a matter of law for the judge, not the jury, to decide. If the ruling cannot be made quickly, the judge will order the jury to retire, and will hear the attorneys' arguments outside the jury's presence.

Whenever the jury leaves the courtroom, the judge will admonish them not to form or express an opinion or discuss the case with anyone.

CLOSING ARGUMENTS. The attorney for the plaintiff or state will present the first argument in closing the case. Generally, he will summarize and comment on the evidence in the most favorable light for his side. He may talk about the facts and properly drawn inferences.

He cannot talk about issues outside the case or about evidence that was not presented. He is not allowed to comment on the defendant's failure to take the stand as a witness in a criminal case.

If he does talk about improper matters, the opposing attorney may object, and the judge will rule on the objection. If the offending remarks are deemed seriously prejudicial, the opposing attorney will ask that the jury be instructed to disregard them, and in some instances may move for a *mistrial,* that is, ask that the present trial be terminated and the case be set for retrial at a later date.

Ordinarily, before closing arguments, the judge will indicate to the attorneys the instructions he will give the jury, and it is proper for the attorneys in closing argument to comment on them and to relate them to the evidence.

The defendant's attorney will next present his arguments. He usually answers statements made in opening argument, points out defects in the plaintiff's case, and summarizes the facts favorable to his client.

Then the plaintiff or state is entitled to the concluding argument to answer the defendant's argument and to make a final appeal to the jury.

If the defendant chooses not to make a closing argument, which sometimes occurs, then the plaintiff or state loses the right to the last argument.

INSTRUCTIONS TO THE JURY. Although giving instructions to the jury is the function of the judge, in many states attorneys for each side submit a number of instructions designed to apply the law to the facts in evidence. The judge will indicate which instructions he will accept and which he will refuse. The attorneys may make objections to such rulings for the purpose of the record in any appeal.

The judge reads these instructions to the jury. This is commonly referred to as the judge's *charge* to the jury. The instructions cover the law as applicable to the case.

In most cases, only the judge may determine what the law is. In some states, however, in criminal cases the jurors are judges of both the facts and the law.

In giving the instructions, the judge will state the issues in the case and define any terms or words necessary. He will tell the jury what it must decide on the issues, if it is to find for the plaintiff or state, or for the defendant. He will advise the jury that it is the sole judge of the facts and of the credibility of witnesses; that upon leaving the courtroom to reach a verdict, it must elect a *foreman* of the jury and then reach a decision based upon the judgment of each individual juror. In some states, the first juror chosen automatically becomes the foreman.

IN THE JURY ROOM. After the instructions, the bailiff will take the jury to the jury room to begin deliberations.

The bailiff will sit outside and not permit anyone to enter or leave the jury room. No one may attempt to *tamper* with the jury in any way while it is deliberating.

Ordinarily, the court furnishes the jury with written forms of all possible verdicts so that when a decision is reached, the jury can choose the proper verdict form.

The decision will be signed by the foreman of the jury and be returned to the courtroom.

Ordinarily, in a criminal case the decision must be unanimous. In some jurisdictions, in civil cases, only nine or ten out of twelve jurors need agree to reach a verdict. However, all federal courts require a unanimous verdict.

If the jurors cannot agree on a verdict, the jury is called a *hung jury*, and the case may be retried before a new jury at a later date.

In some states, the jury may take the judge's instructions and the exhibits introduced in evidence to the jury room.

If necessary, the jury may return to the courtroom in the presence of counsel to ask a question of the judge about his instructions. In such instances, the judge may reread all or certain of the instructions previously given, or supplement or clarify them by further instructions.

If the jury is out overnight, the members often will be housed in a hotel and secluded from all contacts with other persons. In many cases, the jury will be excused to go home at night, especially if there is no objection by either party.

VERDICT. Upon reaching a verdict, the jury returns to the courtroom with the bailiff and, in the presence of the judge, the parties and their respective attorneys, the verdict is read or announced aloud in open court. The reading or announcement may be made by the jury foreman or the court clerk.

Attorneys for either party, but usually the losing party, may ask that the jury be *polled*, in which case each individual juror will be asked if the verdict is his verdict. It is rare for a juror to say that it is not his verdict.

When the verdict is read and accepted by the court, the jury is dismissed, and the trial is concluded.

MOTIONS AFTER VERDICT. Motions permitted to be made after the verdict is rendered will vary from state to state.

A *motion in arrest of judgment* attacks the sufficiency of the indictment or information in a criminal case.

A *motion for judgment non obstante verdicto* may be made after the verdict and before the judgment. This motion requests the judge to enter a judgment for one party, notwithstanding the verdict of the jury in favor of the other side. Ordinarily, this motion raises the same questions as could be raised by a motion for directed verdict.

A *motion for a new trial* sets out alleged errors committed in the trial and asks the trial judge to grant a new trial. In some states, the filing of a motion for a new trial is a condition precedent to an appeal.

JUDGMENT. The verdict of the jury is ineffective until the judge enters *judgment* upon the verdict. In a civil damage action, this judgment might read:
"It is, therefore, ordered, adjudged and decreed that the plaintiff do have and recover the sum of $1,000 of and from the defendant."

At the request of the plaintiff's lawyer, the clerk of the court in such a case will deliver a paper called an *execution* to the sheriff, commanding him to take and sell the property of the defendant and apply the proceeds to the amount of the judgment.

SENTENCING. In a criminal case, if the defendant is convicted, the judge will set a date for sentencing. At that time, the judge may consider mitigating facts in determining the appropriate sentence.

In the great majority of states and in the federal courts, the function of imposing sentence is exclusively that of the judge. But in some states the jury is called upon to determine the sentences for some, or all, crimes, In these states, the judge merely imposes the sentence as determined by the jury.

RIGHTS OF APPEAL. In a civil case, either party may appeal to a higher court. But in a criminal case this right is limited to the defendant. Appeals in either civil or criminal cases may be on such grounds as errors in trial procedure and errors in *substantive law*—that is, in the interpretation of the law by the trial judge. These are the most common grounds for appeals to higher courts, although there are others.

The right of appeal does not extend to the prosecution in a criminal case, even if the prosecutor should discover new evidence of the defendant's guilt after his acquittal. Moreover, the state is powerless to bring the defendant to trial again on the same charge. The U.S. and most state constitutions prevent retrial under provisions known as *double jeopardy* clauses.

Criminal defendants have a further appellate safeguard. Those convicted in state courts may appeal to the federal courts on grounds of violation of constitutional rights, if such grounds exist. This privilege serves to impose the powerful check of the federal judicial system upon abuses that may occur in state criminal procedures.

The record on appeal consists of the papers filed in the trial court and the court reporter's transcript of the evidence. The latter is called a *bill of exceptions* or *transcript on appeal* and must be certified by the trial judge to be true and correct. In most states, only that much of the record need be included as will properly present the questions to be raised on appeal.

APPEAL. Statutes or rules of court provide for procedure on appeals. Ordinarily, the party appealing is called the *appellant*, and the other party the *appellee*.

The appeal is initiated by filing the transcript of the trial court record with the appellate court within the time prescribed. This filing marks the beginning of the time period within which the appellant must file his *brief* setting forth the reasons and the law upon which he relies in seeking a reversal of the trial court.

The appellee then has a specified time within which to file his answer brief. Following this, the appellant may file a second brief, or brief in reply to the appellee's brief.

When the appeal has been fully briefed, the case may be set for hearing on *oral argument* before the appellate court. Sometimes the court itself will ask for argument; otherwise, one of the parties may petition for it. Often, appeals are submitted *on the briefs* without argument.

Courts of appeal do not hear further evidence, and it is unusual for any of the parties to the case to attend the hearing of the oral argument.

Generally, the case has been assigned to one of the judges of the appellate court, although the full court will hear the argument. Thereafter, it is customary for all the judges to confer on the issues presented, and then the judge who has been assigned the case will write an opinion. If a judge or judges disagree with the result, they may dissent and file a *dissenting opinion.* In many states, a written opinion is required.

An appellate court will not weigh evidence and generally will reverse a trial court for errors of law only.

Not every error of law will warrant a reversal. Some are *harmless errors*—that is, the rights of a party to a fair trial were not prejudiced by them.

However, an error of law, such as the admission of improper and persuasive evidence on a material issue, may and often does constitute a *prejudicial* and *reversible error.*

After the opinion is *handed down* and time for the filing of a petition for rehearing—or a petition for transfer, or a petition for *writ of certiorari* (if there is a higher appellate court)—has expired, the appellate court will send its *mandate* to the trial court for further action in the case.

If the lower court is *affirmed,* the case is ended; if reversed, the appellate court may direct that a new trial be held, or that the judgment of the trial court be modified and corrected as prescribed in the opinion.

The taking of an appeal ordinarily does not suspend the operation of a judgment obtained in a civil action in a trial court. Thus, the party prevailing in the trial court may order an execution issued on the judgment, unless the party appealing files an *appeal* or *supersedeas bond,* which binds the party and his surety to pay or perform the judgment in the event it is affirmed on appeal. The filing of this bond will *stay* further action on the judgment until the appeal has been concluded.

23 GLOSSARY OF LEGAL TERMS

accumulative sentence—A sentence, additional to others, imposed at the same time for several distinct offenses; one sentence to begin at the expiration of another.

adjudication—Giving or pronouncing a judgment or decree; also the judgment given.

adversary system—The system of trial practice in the U.S. and some other countries in which each of the opposing, or adversary, parties has full opportunity to present and establish its opposing contentions before the court.

allegation—The assertion, declaration, or statement of a party to an action, made in a pleading, setting out what he expects to prove.

amicus curiae (a-mī′kus kū′ri-ē)—A friend of the court; one who interposes and volunteers information upon some matter of law.

appearance—The formal proceeding by which a defendant submits himself to the jurisdiction of the court.

appellant (a-pel′ant)—The party appealing a decision or judgment to a higher court.

appellate court—A court having jurisdiction of appeal and review; not a "trial court."

arraignment—In criminal practice, to bring a prisoner to the bar of the court to answer to a criminal charge.

This list, which is a sampling of commonly used legal terms, is reprinted by permission of the American Bar Association from *Law and the Courts:* A Layman's Handbook of Court Procedures. The complete booklet is available for 50¢ from the American Bar Association, Circulation Department, 750 North Lake Shore Drive, Chicago, IL 60611. Copyright © 1974 by American Bar Association.

attachment—A remedy by which plaintiff is enabled to acquire a lien upon property or effects of defendant for satisfaction of judgment which plaintiff may obtain in the future.

attorney of record—Attorney whose name appears in the permanent records or files of a case.

bail—To set at liberty a person arrested or imprisoned, on security being taken, for his appearance on a specified day and place.

bail bond—An obligation signed by the accused, with sureties, to secure his presence in court.

bailiff—A court attendant whose duties are to keep order in the courtroom and to have custody of the jury.

best evidence—Primary evidence; the best evidence which is available; any evidence falling short of this standard is secondary; i.e., an original letter is best evidence compared to a copy.

bind over—To hold on bail for trial.

brief—A written or printed document prepared by counsel to file in court, usually setting forth both facts and law in support of his case.

burden of proof—In the law of evidence, the necessity or duty of affirmatively proving a fact or facts in dispute.

cause—A suit, litigation or action—civil or criminal.

certiorari (ser'shi-ō-ra'rī)—An original writ commanding judges or officers of inferior courts to certify or to return records of proceedings in a cause for judicial review.

chambers—Private office or room of a judge.

change of venue—The removal of a suit begun in one county or district, to another, for trial, or from one court to another in the same county or district.

circuit courts—Originally, courts whose jurisdiction extended over several counties or districts, and whose sessions were held in such counties or districts alternately; today, a circuit court may hold all its sessions in one county.

circumstantial evidence—All evidence of indirect nature; the process of decision by which court or jury may reason from circumstances known or proved to establish by inference the principal fact.

codicil (kod'i-sil)—A supplement or an addition to a will.

commit—To send a person to prison, an asylum, workhouse, or reformatory by lawful authority.

common law—Law which derives its authority solely from usages and customs of immemorial antiquity, or from the judgments and decrees of courts. Also called "case law."

commutation—The change of a punishment from a greater degree to a lesser degree, as from death to life imprisonment.

competency—In the law of evidence, the presence of those characteristics which render a witness legally fit and qualified to give testimony.

complainant—Synonymous with "plaintiff."

complaint—The first or initiatory pleading on the part of the complainant, or plaintiff, in a civil action.

concurrent sentence—Sentences for more than one crime in which the time of each is to be served concurrently, rather than successively.

condemnation—The legal process by which real estate of a private owner is taken for public use without his consent, but upon the award and payment of just compensation.

contempt of court—Any act calculated to embarrass, hinder, or obstruct a court in the administration of justice, or calculated to lessen its authority or dignity. Contempts are of two kinds: direct and indirect. Direct contempts are those committed in the immediate presence of the court; indirect is the term chiefly used with reference to the failure or refusal to obey a lawful order.

corpus delicti (kor′pus dē-lik′tī)—The body (material substance) upon which a crime has been committed, e.g., the corpse of a murdered man, the charred remains of a burned house.

corroborating evidence—Evidence supplementary to that already given and tending to strengthen or confirm it.

costs—An allowance for expenses in prosecuting or defending a suit. Ordinarily does not include attorney's fees.

counterclaim—A claim presented by a defendant in opposition to the claim of a plaintiff.

criminal insanity—Lack of mental capacity to do or abstain from doing a particular act; inability to distinguish right from wrong.

cross-examination—The questioning of a witness in a trial, or in the taking of a deposition, by the party opposed to the one who produced the witness.

cumulative sentence—Separate sentences (each additional to the others) imposed against a person convicted upon an indictment containing several counts, each charging a different offense. (Same as accumulative sentence.)

damages—Pecuniary compensation which may be recovered in the courts by any person who has suffered loss, detriment, or injury to his person, property or rights, through the unlawful act or negligence of another.

de novo (dē nō′vō)—Anew, afresh. A "trial de novo" is the retrial of a case.

declaratory judgment—One which declares the rights of the parties or expresses the opinion of the court on a question of law, without ordering anything to be done.

decree—A decision or order of the court. A final decree is one which fully and finally disposes of the litigation; an interlocutory decree is a provisional or preliminary decree which is not final.

default—A "default" in an action of law occurs when a defendant omits to plead within the time allowed or fails to appear at the trial.

demur (dē-mer′)—To file a pleading (called "a demurrer") admitting the truth of the facts in the complaint, or answer, but contending they are legally insufficient.

deposition—The testimony of a witness not taken in open court but in pursuance of authority given by statute or rule of court to take testimony elsewhere.

direct evidence—Proof of facts by witnesses who saw acts done or heard words spoken, as distinguished from circumstantial evidence, which is called indirect.

direct examination—The first interrogation of a witness by the party on whose behalf he is called.

directed verdict—An instruction by the judge to the jury to return a specific verdict.

dismissal without prejudice—Permits the complainant to sue again on the same cause of action, while dismissal "with prejudice" bars the right to bring or maintain an action on the same claim or cause.

double jeopardy—Common-law and constitutional prohibition against more than one prosecution for the same crime, transaction or omission.

due process—Law in its regular course of administration through the courts of justice. The guarantee of due process requires that every man have the protection of a fair trial.

embezzlement—The fraudulent appropriation by a person to his own use or benefit of property or money entrusted to him by another.

eminent domain—The power to take private property for public use by condemnation.

enjoin—To require a person, by writ of injunction from a court of equity, to perform, or to abstain or desist from, some act.

entrapment—The act of officers or agents of a government in inducing a person to commit a crime not contemplated by him, for the purpose of instituting a criminal prosecution against him.

escrow (es′krō)—A writing, or deed, delivered by the grantor into the hands of a third person, to be held by the latter until the happening of a contingency or performance of a condition.

ex post facto (ex pōst fak′to)—After the fact; an act or fact occurring after some previous act or fact, and relating thereto.

exception—A formal objection to an action of the court, during the trial of a case, in refusing a request or overruling an objection; implying that the party excepting does not acquiesce in the decision of the court, but will seek to procure its reversal.

exhibit—A paper, document or other article produced and exhibited to a court during a trial or hearing.

expert evidence—Testimony given in relation to some scientific, technical, or professional matter by experts, i.e., persons qualified to speak authoritatively by reason of their special training, skill, or familiarity with the subject.

extenuating circumstances—Circumstances which render a crime less aggravated, heinous, or reprehensible than it would otherwise be.

extradition—The surrender by one state to another of an individual accused or convicted of an offense outside its own territory, and within the territorial jurisdiction of the other.

fair comment—A term used in the law of libel, applying to statements made by a writer in an honest belief of their truth, relating to official act, even though the statements are not true in fact.

false arrest—Any unlawful physical restraint of another's liberty, whether in prison or elsewhere.

felony—A crime of a graver nature than a misdemeanor. Generally, an offense punishable by death or imprisonment in a penitentiary.

forcible entry and detainer—A summary proceeding for restoring possession of land to one who has been wrongfully deprived of possession.

forgery—The false making or material altering, with intent to defraud, of any writing which, if genuine, might be the foundation of a legal liability.

fraud—An intentional perversion of truth; deceitful practice or device resorted to with intent to deprive another of property or other right, or in some manner to do him injury.

garnishment—A proceeding whereby property, money or credits of a debtor, in possession of another (the garnishee), are applied to the debts of the debtor.

gratuitous guest—In automobile law, a person riding at the invitation of the owner of a vehicle, or his authorized agent, without payment of a consideration or a fare.

guardian ad litem (ad lī′tem)—A person appointed by a court to look after the interests of an infant whose property is involved in litigation.

habeas corpus (hā′ be-as kor′ pus)—"You have the body." The name given a variety of writs whose object is to bring a person before a court or judge. In most common usage, it is directed to the official or person detaining another, commanding him to produce the body of the prisoner or person detained so the court may determine if such person has been denied his liberty without due process of law.

hearsay—Evidence not proceeding from the personal knowledge of the witness.

holographic will (hol-ō-graf′ik)—A testamentary instrument entirely written, dated and signed by the testator in his own handwriting.

hostile witness—A witness who is subject to cross-examination by the party who called him to testify, because of his evident antagonism toward that party as exhibited in his direct examination.

hypothetical question—A combination of facts and circumstances, assumed or proved, stated in such a form as to constitute a coherent state of facts upon which the opinion of an expert can be asked by way of evidence in a trial.

impeachment of witness—An attack on the credibility of a witness by the testimony of other witnesses.

inadmissible—That which, under the established rules of evidence, cannot be admitted or received.

in camera (in kam' e-ra)—In chambers; in private.

incompetent evidence—Evidence which is not admissible under the established rules of evidence.

indeterminate sentence—An indefinite sentence of "not less than" and "not more than" so many years, the exact term to be served being afterwards determined by parole authorities within the minimum and maximum limits set by the court or by statute.

indictment—An accusation in writing found and presented by a grand jury, charging that a person therein named has done some act, or been guilty of some omission, which, by law, is a crime.

injunction—A mandatory or prohibitive writ issued by a court.

instruction—A direction given by the judge to the jury concerning the law of the case.

interlocutory—Provisional; temporary; not final. Refers to orders and decrees of a court.

interrogatories—Written questions propounded by one party and served on an adversary, who must provide written answers thereto under oath.

intervention—A proceeding in a suit or action by which a third person is permitted by the court to make himself a party.

intestate—One who dies without leaving a will.

irrelevant—Evidence not relating or applicable to the matter in issue; not supporting the issue.

jury—A certain number of persons, selected according to law, and sworn to inquire of certain matters of fact, and declare the truth upon evidence laid before them.

grand jury—A jury of inquiry whose duty is to receive complaints and accusations in criminal cases, hear the evidence and find bills of indictment in cases where they are satisfied that there is probable cause that a crime was committed and that a trial ought to be held.

petit jury—The ordinary jury of twelve (or fewer) persons for the trial of a civil or criminal case. So called to distinguish it from the grand jury.

leading question—One which instructs a witness how to answer or puts into his mouth words to be echoed back; one which suggests to the witness the answer desired. Prohibited on direct examination.

libel—A method of defamation expressed by print, writing, pictures, or signs. In its most general sense, any publication that is injurious to the reputation of another.

limitation—A certain time allowed by statute in which litigation must be brought.

malfeasance (mal-fē′zans)—Evil doing; ill conduct; the commission of some act which is positively prohibited by law.

mandamus (man-dā′mus)—The name of a writ which issues from a court of superior jurisdiction, directed to an inferior court, commanding the performance of a particular act.

mandate—A judicial command or precept proceeding from a court or judicial officer, directing the proper officer to enforce a judgment, sentence, or decree.

manslaughter—The unlawful killing of another without malice; may be either voluntary, upon a sudden impulse, or involuntary in the commission of some unlawful act.

material evidence—Such as is relevant and goes to the substantial issues in dispute.

misdemeanor—Offenses less than felonies; generally those punishable by fine or imprisonment otherwise than in penitentiaries.

misfeasance—A misdeed or trespass; the improper performance of some act which a person may lawfully do.

mistrial—An erroneous or invalid trial; a trial which cannot stand in law because of lack of jurisdiction, wrong drawing of jurors, or disregard of some other fundamental requisite.

mitigating circumstance—One which does not constitute a justification or excuse for an offense, but which may be considered as reducing the degree of moral culpability.

moot—Unsettled; undecided. A moot point is one not settled by judicial decisions.

moral turpitude—Conduct contrary to honesty, modesty, or good morals.

murder—The unlawful killing of a human being by another with malice aforethought, either expressed or implied.

negligence—The failure to do something which a reasonable man, guided by ordinary considerations, would do; or the doing of something which a reasonable and prudent man would not do.

nolo contendere (nō'lō kon-ten'de-rē)—A pleading usually used by defendants in criminal cases, which literally means "I will not contest it."

objection—The act of taking exception to some statement or procedure in trial. Used to call the court's attention to improper evidence or procedure.

of counsel—A phrase commonly applied to counsel employed to assist in the preparation or management of the case, or its presentation on appeal, but who is not the principal attorney of record.

out of court—One who has no legal status in court is said to be "out of court," i.e., he is not before the court. For example, when a plaintiff, by some act of omission or commission, shows that he is unable to maintain his action, he is frequently said to have put himself "out of court."

panel—A list of jurors to serve in a particular court, or for the trial of a particular action; denotes either the whole body of persons summoned as jurors for a particular term of court or those selected by the clerk by lot.

parole—The conditional release from prison of a convict before the expiration of his sentence. If he observes the conditions, the parolee need not serve the remainder of his sentence.

parties—The persons who are actively concerned in the prosecution or defense of a legal proceeding.

peremptory challenge—The challenge which the prosecution or defense may use to reject a certain number of prospective jurors without assigning any cause.

plaintiff—A person who brings an action; the party who complains or sues in a personal action and is so named on the record.

plaintiff in error—The party who obtains a writ of error to have a judgment or other proceeding at law reviewed by an appellate court.

pleading—The process by which the parties in a suit or action alternately present written statements of their contentions, each responsive to that which precedes, and each serving to narrow the field of controversy, until there evolves a single point, affirmed on one side and denied on the other, called the "issue" upon which they then go to trial.

polling the jury—A practice whereby the jurors are asked individually whether they assented, and still assent, to the verdict.

power of attorney—An instrument authorizing another to act as one's agent or attorney.

prejudicial error—Synonymous with "reversible error"; an error which warrants the appellate court to reverse the judgment before it.

preliminary hearing—Synonymous with "preliminary examination"; the hearing given a person charged with a crime by a magistrate or judge to determine whether he should be held for trial. Since the Constitution states that a man cannot be accused in secret, a preliminary hearing is open to the public unless the defendant himself requests that it be closed. The accused person must be present at this hearing and must be accompanied by his attorney.

presumption of fact—An inference as to the truth or falsity of any proposition of fact, drawn by a process of reasoning in the absence of actual certainty of its truth or falsity, or until such certainty can be ascertained.

presumption of law—A rule of law that courts and judges shall draw a particular inference from a particular fact, or from particular evidence.

probate—The act or process of proving a will.

probation—In modern criminal administration, allowing a person convicted of some minor offense (particularly juvenile offenders) to go at large, under a suspension of sentence, during good behavior, and generally under the supervision or guardianship of a probation officer.

prosecutor—One who instigates the prosecution upon which an accused is arrested or one who brings an accusation against the party whom he suspects to be guilty; also, one who takes charge of a case and performs the function of trial lawyer for the people.

quash—To overthrow; vacate; to annul or void a summons or indictment.

quasi judicial (kwā'sī)—Authority or discretion vested in an officer, wherein his acts partake of a judicial character.

reasonable doubt—An accused person is entitled to acquittal if, in the minds of the jury, his guilt has not been proved beyond a "reasonable doubt"; that state of the minds of jurors in which they cannot say they feel an abiding conviction as to the truth of the charge.

rebuttal—The introduction of rebutting evidence; the showing that statements of witnesses as to what occurred is not true; the stage of a trial at which such evidence may be introduced.

redirect examination—Follows cross-examination and is exercised by the party who first examined the witness.

referee—A person to whom a cause pending in a court is referred by the court to take testimony, hear the parties, and report thereon to the court. He is an officer exercising judicial powers and is an arm of the court for a specific purpose.

rest—A party is said to "rest" or "rest his case" when he has presented all the evidence he intends to offer.

retainer—Act of the client in employing his attorney or counsel, and also denotes the fee which the client pays when he retains the attorney to act for him.

search and seizure, unreasonable—In general, an examination without authority of law of one's premises or person with a view to discovering stolen contraband or illicit property or some evidence of guilt to be used in prosecuting a crime.

search warrant—An order in writing, issued by a justice or magistrate, in the name of the state, directing an officer to search a specified house or other premises for stolen property. Usually required as a condition precedent to a legal search and seizure.

self-defense—The protection of one's person or property against some injury attempted by another. The law of "self defense" justifies an act done in the reasonable belief of immediate danger. When acting in justifiable self-defense, a person may not be punished criminally nor held responsible for civil damages.

separate maintenance—Allowance granted for support to a married party, and any children, while the party is living apart from the spouse, but not divorced.

slander—Base and defamatory spoken words tending to harm another's reputation, business or means of livelihood. Both "libel" and "slander" are methods of defamation—the former being expressed by print, writings, pictures or signs; the latter orally.

state's evidence—Testimony given by an accomplice or participant in a crime, tending to convict others.

statute—The written law in contradistinction to the unwritten law.

stay—A stopping or arresting of a judicial proceeding by order of the court.

stipulation—An agreement by attorneys on opposite sides of a case as to any matter pertaining to the proceedings or trial. It is not binding unless assented to by the parties, and most stipulations must be in writing.

subpoena (su-pē′nä)—A process to cause a witness to appear and give testimony before a court or magistrate.

subpoena duces tecum (su-pē′nä dū′sēz tē′kum)—A process by which the court commands a witness to produce certain documents or records in a trial.

summons—A writ directing the sheriff or other officer to notify the named person that an action has been commenced against him in court and that he is required to appear, on the day named, and answer the complaint in such action.

testimony—Evidence given by a competent witness, under oath; as distinguished from evidence derived from writings and other sources.

tort—An injury or wrong committed, either with or without force, to the person or property of another.

transcript—The official record of proceedings in a trial or hearing.

trial de novo (dē nō′vō)—A new trial or retrial held in a higher court in which the whole case is gone into as if no trial had been held in a lower court.

true bill—In criminal practice, the endorsement made by a grand jury upon a bill of indictment when they find sufficient evidence to warrant a criminal charge.

undue influence—Whatever destroys free will and causes a person to do something he would not do if left to himself.

venire (vē-nī'rē)—Technically, a writ summoning persons to court to act as jurors; popularly used as meaning the body of names thus summoned.

veniremen (vē-nī'rē-men)—Members of a panel of jurors.

venue (ven'ū)—The particular county, city or geographical area in which a court with jurisdiction may hear and determine a case.

verdict—In practice, the formal and unanimous decision or finding made by a jury, reported to the court and accepted by it.

waiver of immunity—A means authorized by statutes by which a witness, in advance of giving testimony or producing evidence, may renounce the fundamental right guaranteed by the Constitution that no person shall be compelled to be a witness against himself.

warrant of arrest—A writ issued by a magistrate, justice, or other competent authority, to a sheriff, or other officer, requiring him to arrest a person therein named and bring him before the magistrate or court to answer to a specified charge.

weight of evidence—The balance or preponderance of evidence; the inclination of the greater amount of credible evidence, offered in a trial, to support one side of the issue rather than the other.

willful—A "willful" act is one done intentionally, without justifiable cause, as distinguished from an act done carelessly or inadvertently.

with prejudice—The term, as applied to judgment of dismissal, is as conclusive of rights of parties as if action had been prosecuted to final adjudication adverse to the plaintiff.

without prejudice—A dismissal "without prejudice" allows a new suit to be brought on the same cause of action.

witness—One who testifies to what he has seen, heard, or otherwise observed.

writ—An order issuing from a court of justice and requiring the performance of a specified act, or giving authority and commission to have it done.

REFERENCE BOOKS
FOR MYSTERY WRITERS

ACKROYD, JAMES. *The Investigator.* Frederick Muller, Ltd.

BARZUN, JACQUES, and TAYLOR, WENDELL HERTIG. *A Catalogue of Crime.* New York: Harper & Row, 1971.

BRIDGES, B. C. *Practical Fingerprinting.* Revised by CHARLES E. O'HARA, with a foreword by AUGUST VOLLMER. New York: Funk & Wagnalls, 1963.

CAPUTO, RUDOLPH R. *Criminal Interrogation.* Springfield, IL: Charles C. Thomas.

CHAPPELL, DUNCAN, and FOGARTY, FAITH. *Forcible Rape: A Literature Review and Annotated Bibliography.* (National Institute of Law Enforcement and Criminal Justice, Law Enforcement Assistance Administration, U.S. Dept. of Justice.) Washington, D.C.: Government Printing Office, 1978.

CUNLIFFE, FREDERICK, and PIAZZA, PETER B. *Criminalistics and Scientific Investigation.* Englewood Cliffs, N.J.: Prentice-Hall, 1980.

DEFOREST, PETER R., GAENSSLEN, R. E., and LEE, HENRY C. *Forensic Science: An Introduction to Criminalistics.* New York: McGraw-Hill, 1983.

DIENSTEIN, WILLIAM. *Technics for Crime Investigation.* Springfield, IL: Charles C. Thomas.

FITZGERALD, MAURICE. *Handbook of Criminal Investigation.* New York: Arco.

FOX, RICHARD H., and CUNNINGHAM, CARL L. *Crime Scene Search and Physical Evidence Handbook.* (U.S. Dept. of Justice, Law Enforcement Assistance Administration, National Institute of Law Enforcement and Criminal Justice.) Washington, D.C.: Government Printing Office, 1973.

GODDARD, KENNETH WILLIAM. *Crime Scene Investigation.* Reston, VA.: Reston Publishing Co., 1977.

HAGEN, ORDEAN A. *Who Done It? A Guide to Detective, Mystery and Suspense Fiction.* New York: R. R. Bowker, 1969.

HALL, ANGUS (ed.). *The Crime Busters: The FBI, Scotland Yard,*

Interpol: The Story of Criminal Detection. London: Verdict Press, 1976.

KEATING, H. R. F. (ed.). *Whodunit? A Guide to Crime, Suspense & Spy Fiction.* New York: Van Nostrand Reinhold, 1982.

KINCHUM, MOORE E. *How to Become a Successful Private Eye.* Summit, PA: TAB Books.

KIRK, PAUL LELAND. *Crime Investigation* (2nd ed.). Edited by JOHN I. THORNTON. New York: Wiley, 1974.

——. *Crime Investigation; Physical Evidence and the Police Laboratory.* New York: Interscience Publishers, 1953.

LAURIE, PETER. *Scotland Yard. A Study of the Metropolitan Police.* New York: Holt, Rinehart and Winston, 1970.

O'HARA, CHARLES P. *Fundamentals of Criminal Investigation.* Springfield, IL: Charles C. Thomas, 1966.

PENZLER, OTTO (ed.). *Detectionary.* Woodstock, N.Y.: Overlook Press, 1977.

RAPP, BURT. *Shadowing and Surveillance: A Complete Guide Book.* Port Townsend, WA: Loompanics. 1985.

RAPP, BURT. *Undercover Work.* Port Townsend, WA: Loompanics, 1985.

SCHULTZ, DONALD O. *Crime Scene Investigation.* Englewood Cliffs, N.J.: Prentice-Hall, 1977.

SMITH, MYRON J. *Cloak and Dagger Fiction: An Annotated Guide to Spy Thrillers* (2nd ed.). Santa Barbara: ABC-Clio, 1982

SÖDERMAN, HARRY, and O'CONNELL, JOHN J. *Modern Criminal Investigation* (5th ed.). Revised by CHARLES E. O'HARA. New York: Funk & Wagnalls, 1962.

STEINBRUNNER, CHRIS, and PENZLER, OTTO (eds.) *Encyclopedia of Mystery and Detection.* New York: Harvest/HBJ, 1984.

——. *Trial Evidence and Effective Litigation Techniques in Federal and State Courts.* American Law Institute.

WAGNER, DIANE. *Corpus Delicti.* New York: St. Martin's Press. 1986.

SPECIAL NOTE: Since the laws vary widely from state to state, writers are advised to consult the reference books that give information about the particular state in which a crime or trial or investigation takes place. Criminal law, criminal codes and procedures are usually available at a State Law Library, business library, or university law school, and should be carefully checked to be sure that the factual background used in a mystery novel or short story is authentic.

ABOUT THE AUTHORS

The range of books by British Author JOAN AIKEN is impressive by any standard: Her novels for adults as well as those for children and teenagers have won critical acclaim on both sides of the Atlantic—all of them praised for the ingenuity in plotting, realism in characterization, and unrelenting suspense. Her most recent titles include *Blackground, If I Were You* (both adult novels); *The Haunting of Lamb House* (a triple ghost story in which Henry James is one of the heroes); *Return to Harken House* (a spooky young adult novella); and several collections of short stories for children—*A Foot in the Grave, The Last Slice of Rainbow,* and *A Whisper in the Night: Tales of Terror and Suspense.*

A four-time Edgar Allan Poe nominee, British crime fiction writer ROBERT BARNARD is the author of many novels, including the recently published *A City of Strangers, At Death's Door,* and *The Skeleton in the Grass,* among others. His wry wit and sense of the comic are hallmarks of his fiction, though never to the point of overshadowing the mystery and menace and distinguished writing style that characterize his work. In addition to his novels, he has written numerous short mystery stories, one of which—"The Woman in the Wardrobe" (his tenth to appear in *Ellery Queen's Mystery Magazine*)—won the annual *EQMM* Readers' Award. A collection of his short stories, *Death of a Salesperson,* was recently published.

REX BURNS established himself as a top writer of detective novels with the publication of the first in his Gabe Wager series, *The Alvarez Journal* (1975), for which he won the Edgar (given by the Mystery Writers of America) for "Best First Mystery." Several Gabe Wager novels have followed, including *The Killing Zone* and *The Avenging Angel,* which was made into a movie starring Charles Bronson. He recently launched a new series, featuring private detective Devlin Kirk, with *Suicide Season* and the recent *Parts Unknown.* His story, "The Mirrored Badge," is included in

Scribner's 1986 *Colloquium on Crime,* and he served as co-editor of an anthology of mystery stories recently published by Viking. A scholar as well as a fiction writer, Mr. Burns is professor of American Literature at the University of Colorado, at Denver, and served as Fulbright lecturer in Greece and Argentina.

MAX BYRD is the author of four thrillers featuring Mike Haller, a "hard-boiled, egg-headed private detective." These include *Fly Away, Jill,* the prize-winning *California Thriller, Finders Weepers,* and most recently, *Fuse Time,* published by Bantam Books. He is a Professor of English at the University of California at Davis and a member of its Creative Writing Program.

Of the more than eighty published books MARY BLOUNT CHRISTIAN has to her credit, forty-five of them are mysteries for children, many under such series headings as Goosehill Gang, Sebastian (Super Sleuth), The Determined Detectives, the Sherlock Street Investigators, and Undercover Kids. Her many literary prizes and honors include the Mystery Writers of America's Edgar Allan Poe Scroll for her easy-reading book, *The Doggone Mystery,* the Catholic Library Association's (Bishop Byrne Chapter) Ann Martin Award for a body of work; and the Silver Burdett & Ginn World of Reading Readers' Choice for *Nothing Much Happened Today,* selected by nationwide classroom voting.

Several of her books have been Junior Literary Guild and Book-of-the-Month Club selections, have been named "Pick of Lists" by the American Booksellers Association, "Best Books of the Year" by R. R. Bowker and the Child Study Association, and Classroom Choices by the Children's Book Council. Five of her Goosehill Gang mysteries have been made into movies, and others into film strips and recordings. Her work has been translated into French, Swedish, Japanese, and German, and is also available in Braille.

During his forty-year career as a full-time writer of mystery fiction, the late STANLEY ELLIN established himself as one of the leading writers in the field. From the publication of his very first story in 1948—"The Specialty of the House," published in *Ellery Queen's Mystery Magazine,* for which he won their short story prize (as did his subsequent six stories)—he went on to receive honor after honor. He was awarded three Edgars from The Mystery Writers of America—two for "Best Short Story" and one for his now classic novel, *The Eighth Circle* (1958). In 1975 he was awarded France's Grand Prix de Littérature Policière for his novel, *Mirror, Mirror on the Wall,* and in 1981 he received the Mystery Writers of America Grand Master Award for lifetime achievement.

Several of his novels were made into motion pictures (*House of Cards*; *Leda*, based on *The Key to Nicholas Street*; and *The Big Night*, based on *Dreadful Summit*), starring Orson Welles, Jean-Paul Belmondo, and John Barrymore, respectively.

A prolific writer of mystery and detective fiction, LOREN D. ESTLEMAN has won wide recognition for his Amos Walker private eye series, with such titles as *The Glass Highway*, *The Midnight Man*, *Motor City Blues*, *Angel Eyes*, and *Sweet Women Lie*, all published by Houghton Mifflin. His short mystery stories, which appear in such publications as *Alfred Hitchcock's Mystery Magazine*, have garnered many prizes, including two Shamus Awards given by the Private Eye Writers of America. His new novel *Whiskey River*, a Bantam hardcover, is the first in a projected trilogy about the history of crime in Detroit.

Mr. Estleman writes with equal success in the western field, to which he has contributed such popular titles as *The Hider*, *The High Rocks*, *Stamping Ground*, and *Aces and Eights* (all published by Doubleday), the last of these winner of the Golden Spur Award made annually by the Western Writers of America. Two others, *This Old Bill* (Doubleday) and *Bloody Season* (Bantam), were nominated for the Pulitzer Prize.

SUE GRAFTON is the author of seven mystery novels featuring female private eye Kinsey Millhone: *"A" Is for Alibi*, *"B" Is for Burglar* (winner of both the Shamus and Anthony awards), *"C" Is for Corpse* (winner of the Anthony Award), *"D" Is for Deadbeat*, *"E" Is for Evidence*, *"F" Is for Fugitive*, and *"G" Is for Gumshoe*. She has also written seven Kinsey Millhone short stories. Since 1982, Ms. Grafton and her husband, Steven Humphrey, have collaborated on numerous movies for television, including two Agatha Christie adaptations, "A Caribbean Mystery" and "Sparkling Cyanide."

The hallmark of MARTHA GRIMES' impressive list of mystery novels can be found in their titles—each bears the name of a British pub and is written in the tradition of such British mystery novelists as Agatha Christie, Margery Allingham, and Dorothy L. Sayers, though she herself is an American. Her most recent mystery is *The Old Silent*, a selection of the Literary Guild, the Mystery Guild, and the Doubleday Book Club. Her earlier books include *The Man with a Load of Mischief*, *The Five Bells and Bladebone*, *I Am the Only Running Footman*, *The Old Fox Deceiv'd*, *Help the Poor Struggler*, all published by Little, Brown and all featuring Superintendent Richard Jury and his amateur friend-in-detection, Melrose Plant. She has also written a mystery in verse, *Send Bygraves.*

JEREMIAH HEALY is a graduate of Rutgers College and Harvard Law School. In 1978, he joined the faculty of New England School of Law in Boston, becoming a full professor in 1983. His first novel, *Blunt Darts,* was selected by *The New York Times* as one of the seven best mysteries of 1984. Healy's second book, *The Staked Goat,* received the "Shamus" award from the Private Eye Writers of America as the Best Novel of 1986. His third and fourth books, *So Like Sleep* and *Swan Dive,* were published in 1987 and 1988. A fifth, *Yesterday's News,* appeared from Harper & Row in July, 1989.

Healy has served as vice-president of the Private Eye Writers of America and as a committee chair for the Mystery Writers of America "Edgar" awards. He has spoken on mystery writing at numerous events, including *The Boston Globe* Book Festival Banquet, the Harvard Bookstore Cafe/Boston Public Library Author Series, the International Congress of Crime Writers, Semana Negra in Spain, and the last four Bouchercons.

TONY HILLERMAN is the author of sixteen books, both fiction and nonfiction. He is best known for ten mystery novels involving the Navajo Tribal Police and the Navajo people. These books have been published in eleven languages, from Japanese to Hebrew, and the latest two *(Talking God* and *Thief of Time)* were national best sellers. His earlier works include *Dance Hall of the Dead,* winner of the 1974 Edgar Allan Poe Award; *Skinwalkers,* which won the Western Writers of America Golden Spur Award of 1988 as the best novel involving Western culture; *Fly on the Wall,* republished by Garland in its "Fifty Classics of Crime Fiction" series; and *Boy Who Made Dragonfly,* honored by the Western Writers of America for children's literature.

British mystery writer P.D. JAMES, one of the best-selling mystery writers in the world and creator of the "intellectual detective" Adam Dalgliesh, is the author of eleven crime novels, most recently *Devices and Desires,* published by Knopf. Her earlier books, many of which have been adapted for television, include *A Taste for Death, The Black Tower, An Unsuitable Job for a Woman, Innocent Blood,* and *The Skull Beneath the Skin.*

British novelist PETER LOVESEY is the author of fourteen crime novels and a number of short stories published in *Ellery Queen's Mystery Magazine.* His novels include *Wobble to Death,* winner of the British (Panther/Macmillan) award for a first crime novel;

Waxwork, which won the Silver Dagger of the Crime Writers' Association of Great Britain; *The False Inspector Dew,* which won the Gold Dagger; and his recent *Bertie and the Seven Bodies,* which was a Mystery Guild selection. His Victorian crime novels serve as the basis of the popular TV series *Mystery!,* featuring Sergeant Cribb.

PATRICIA MOYES is the author of eighteen best-selling mystery novels featuring Chief Superintendent Henry Tibbett of Scotland Yard, the newest called *Black Girl, White Girl.* Her earlier titles include *Murder à la Mode, Death on the Agenda, Falling Star, Johnny Underground, Murder Fantastical, Death and the Dutch Uncle, Dead Men Don't Ski, Down Among the Dead Men, Many Deadly Returns, Season of Snow and Sins, The Curious Affair of the Third Dog, Black Widower, The Coconut Killings, Who is Simon Warwick?, Angel Death,* and *A Six-Letter Word for Death,* all published by Holt, Rinehart, and Winston.

Three of her novels were published in an anthology under the name of *Murder by 3's,* and nine of her books have been reissued by Owl Paperbacks, among them *Death on the Agenda, Dead Men Don't Ski,* and *Murder Fantastical.* Her books have been translated into eleven languages, and many have been serialized in England, the United States, Canada, Holland, Germany, Brazil, and Italy.

MARCIA MULLER's mystery novel series starring detective Sharon McCone meets with increasingly popular and critical acclaim. One critic comments about *There's Something in a Sunday* (Mysterious Press), "It pulls together the skeins of her plot very neatly." Her other novels (not all featuring Sharon McCone) include *There Hangs the Knife, Eye of the Storm, The Cavalier in White, Leave a Message for Willie, The Tree of Death, Ask the Cards a Question, The Shape of Dread,* and *Dark Star.*

She has also collaborated with Bill Pronzini on several novels and anthologies, among them *The Deadly Arts, The Wickedest Show on Earth, Dark Lessons, Chapter and Hearse,* and *The Web She Weaves.* Her short stories have been published in various magazines and anthologies.

Under her two pseudonyms, Barbara Michaels and ELIZABETH PETERS, Barbara Mertz has written over forty novels of mystery and suspense, in addition to two nonfiction books on Egyptology under her own name. She earned her Ph.D. at the University of Chicago. In 1986 she was awarded the Anthony "Grandmaster" award at Bouchercon (an annual convention of mystery fans, writers, and publishers) and in 1989 she was guest of honor at the first Malice Domestic Convention, a gathering of fans of the traditional mystery novel. As Barbara Michaels, her most recently published book is *Smoke and Mirrors*, which was a Literary Guild and Doubleday Book Club selection. A new Barbara Michaels, *Into the Darkness*, will be published by Simon and Schuster in 1990. The most recent Elizabeth Peters book is *Naked Once More*, published by Warner and featuring one of her series characters, the acerbic and quick-witted Jacqueline Kirby. She is presently working on a new novel featuring her most popular characters, the Victorian archaeologists Amelia Peabody and her husband Emerson, whose last appearance was in *Deeds of the Disturber*.

A full-time professional writer since 1969, BILL PRONZINI has published (alone and in collaboration with others) more than forty novels, three nonfiction books, four collections of short stories, and some 275 uncollected stories, articles, essays, and book reviews. He has also edited or co-edited upwards of sixty anthologies in a variety of different fields. His most recent books are *Jackpot* (Delacorte, 1990), the 17th novel in his popular "Nameless Detective" series, and *The Best Western Stories of Bill Pronzini* (Ohio University Press/Swallow Press, 1990). Among his published fiction are more than a score of locked-room and impossible crime stories, several of which have been anthologized ("Proof of Guilt" five times), and three novels which have "impossible" plots.

British fiction writer IAN STUART is the author of numerous short mystery stories that have appeared in *Ellery Queen's Mystery Magazine* and reprinted in anthologies in magazines in the United States and Great Britain. He is also the author of nineteen crime novels, fifteen under his own name (most recently *Master Plan, Sandscreen*, and *The Margin*) and four under his pseudonym Malcolm Gray (*A Matter of Principle, An Unwelcome Presence*, etc.). Nine of his novels have been published by Doubleday, and several have been Detective Book Club selections.

Mr. Stuart has also written a nonfiction book on golf and a large number of magazine articles.

Author of nine mystery novels featuring his lawyer/detective Brady Coyne, WILLIAM G. TAPPLY has won high critical praise for his deft, believable characterization of people "you can see and hear, and understand what makes them tick." His most recent novels, *Client Privilege* and *Dead Winter* (both published by Delacorte), follow *A Void in Hearts, The Vulgar Boatman, Dead Meat, The Marine Corpse, Follow the Sharks, The Dutch Blue*

Error, and *Death at Charity's Point,* all published by Scribner's. *Death at Charity's Point* also won the Scribner Crime Novel Award for the best first novel of 1984. Mr. Tapply is Contributing Editor for *Field & Stream* Magazine, and has published more than 100 articles and short stories in such magazines as *Sports Illustrated, Newsweek, Reader's Digest, Yankee, Outdoor Life, Better Homes & Gardens, Organic Gardening,* and *Ellery Queen's Mystery Magazine.* He is also the author of two nonfiction books: his most recent, *Opening Day and Other Neuroses* (Lyons & Burford) is on fishing; *Those Hours Spent Outdoors,* a collection of hunting and fishing essays, was published by Scribner's in 1988.

British novelist MICHAEL UNDERWOOD draws on his long experience as a barrister on the staff of the Public Prosecutor in London for his more than 45 crime novels, most of them published in the United States under the St. Martin's Press imprint. His recent titles include *Rosa's Dilemma, A Compelling Case, The Uninvited Corpse, Dual Enigma, The Injudicious Judge,* and *The Hidden Man,* all impressive for their authentic police procedure and courtroom scenes. One of his most engaging series sleuths is British solicitor Rosa Epton.

The Uninvited Corpse was a selection of the Detective Book Club (as were 16 of his earlier novels) and a Book-of-the-Month Club Alternate. His novel, *Hand of Fate,* was published by Harper and Row in its Perennial British Mystery series.

The publication of PHYLLIS A. WHITNEY's novel, *The Singing Stones,* brings to 34 the total number of her adult suspense novels, in addition to numerous mysteries and novels for young people. Her earlier works include the best-selling *Rainbow in the Mist, Feather on the Moon, Silversword, Flaming Tree, Dream of Orchids, Rainsong, Vermilion,* and *Emerald,* all of which were Literary Guild Selections. Paperback sales of her adult novels have passed forty million copies. She received the 1988 Grandmaster Award for lifetime achievement from the Mystery Writers of America, an organization she served as president in 1975.

She is also author of *Guide to Fiction Writing* and *Writing Juvenile Stories and Novels,* both published by The Writer, Inc.